David Schloss

Olympus EVOLT E-510

Magic Lantern Guides®

OLYMPUS®

EVOLT E-510

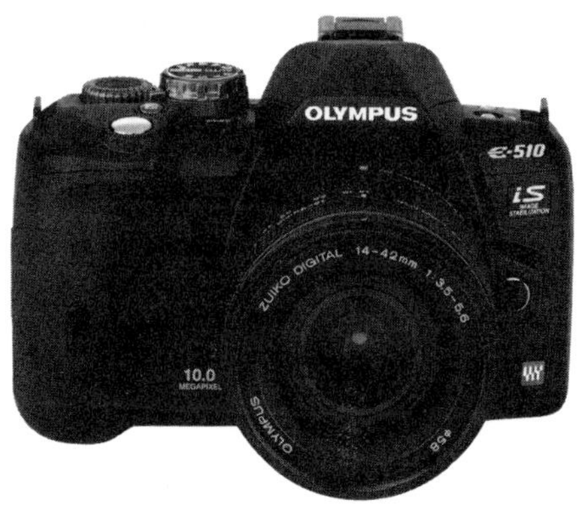

David Schloss

LARK BOOKS
A Division of Sterling Publishing Co., Inc.
New York / London

Book Design and Layout: Michael Robertson
Cover Design: Thom Gaines – Electron Graphics
Associate Art Director: Lance Wille

10 9 8 7 6 5 4 3 2 1

First Edition

Published by Lark Books, A Division of Sterling Publishing Co., Inc.
387 Park Avenue South, New York, N.Y. 10016

Distributed in Canada by Sterling Publishing,
c/o Canadian Manda Group, 165 Dufferin Street
Toronto, Ontario, Canada M6K 3H6

Distributed in the United Kingdom by GMC Distribution Services,
Castle Place, 166 High Street, Lewes, East Sussex, England BN7 1XU

Distributed in Australia by Capricorn Link (Australia) Pty Ltd.,
P.O. Box 704, Windsor, NSW 2756 Australia

If you have questions or comments about this book, please contact:
Lark Books
67 Broadway
Asheville, NC 28801
(828) 253-0467

Manufactured in USA

ISBN 13: 978-1-60059-257-7
ISBN 10: 1-60059-257-0

For information about custom editions, special sales, premium and corporate purchases, please contact Sterling Special Sales Department at 800-805-5489 or specialsales@sterlingpub.com

Contents

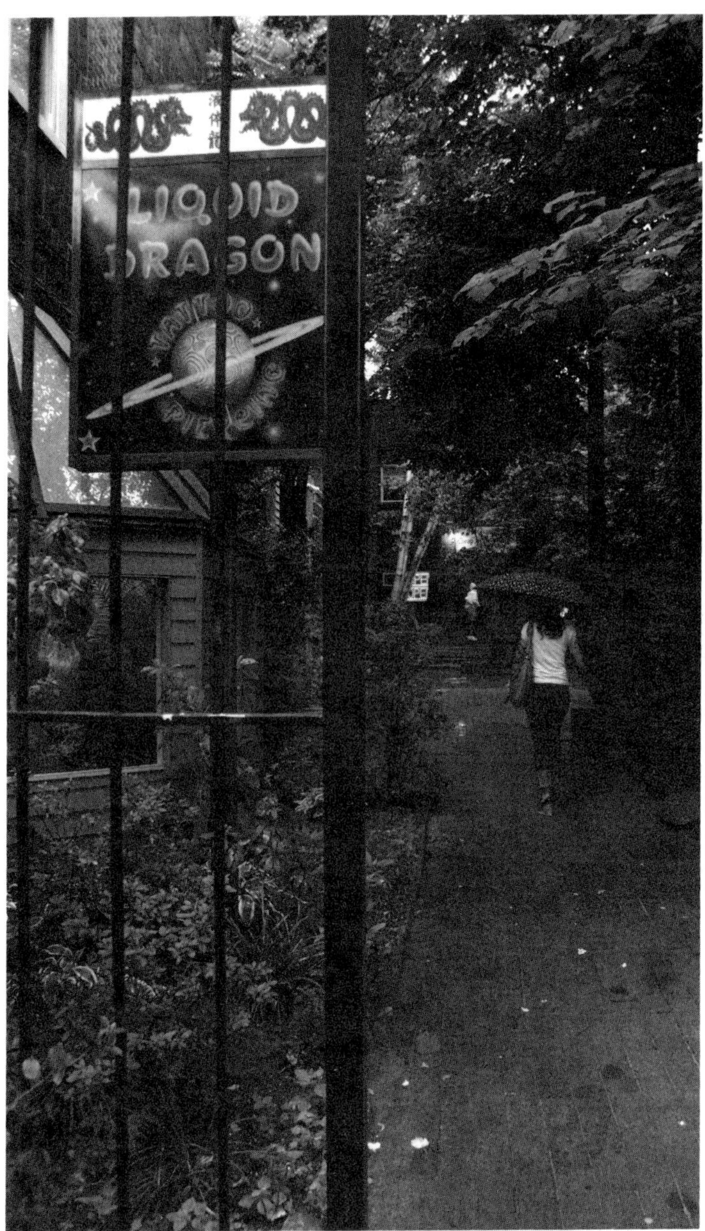

Photo ©Kara Helmkamp

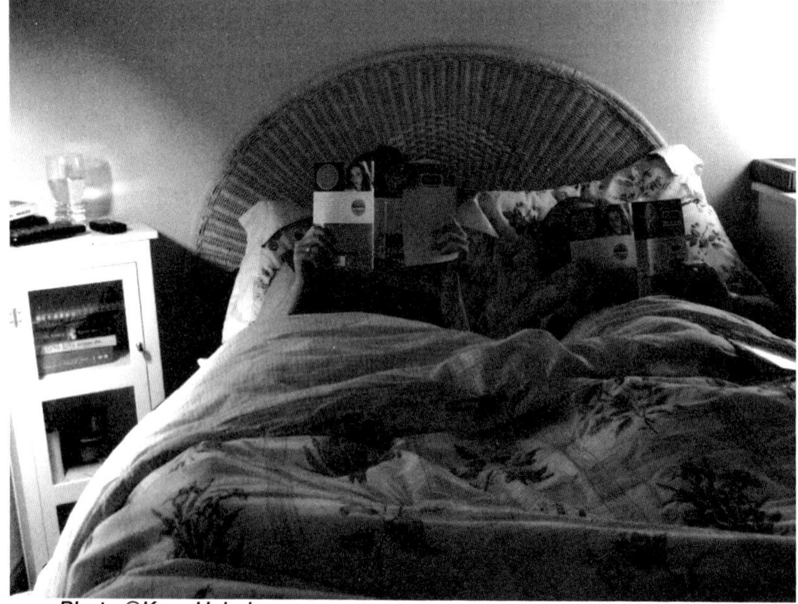

Photo ©Kara Helmkamp

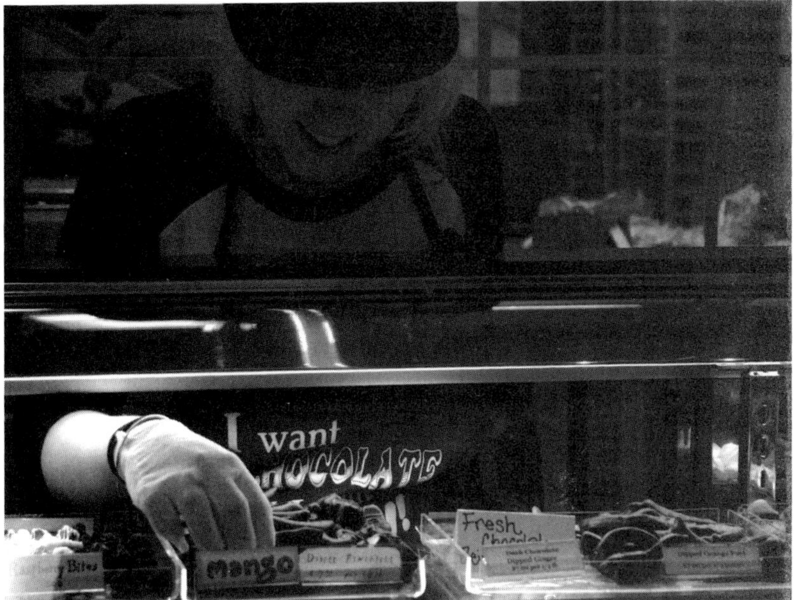

Photo ©Kara Helmkamp

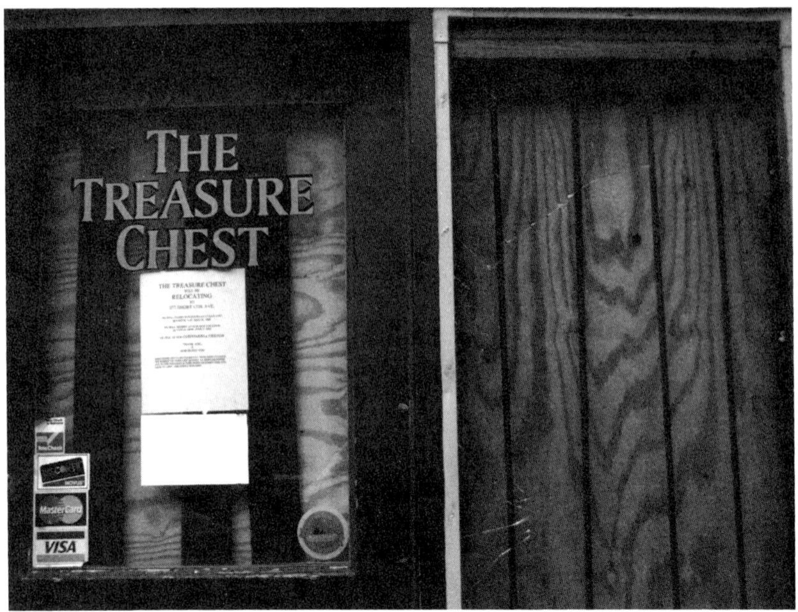

Photo ©Kara Helmkamp

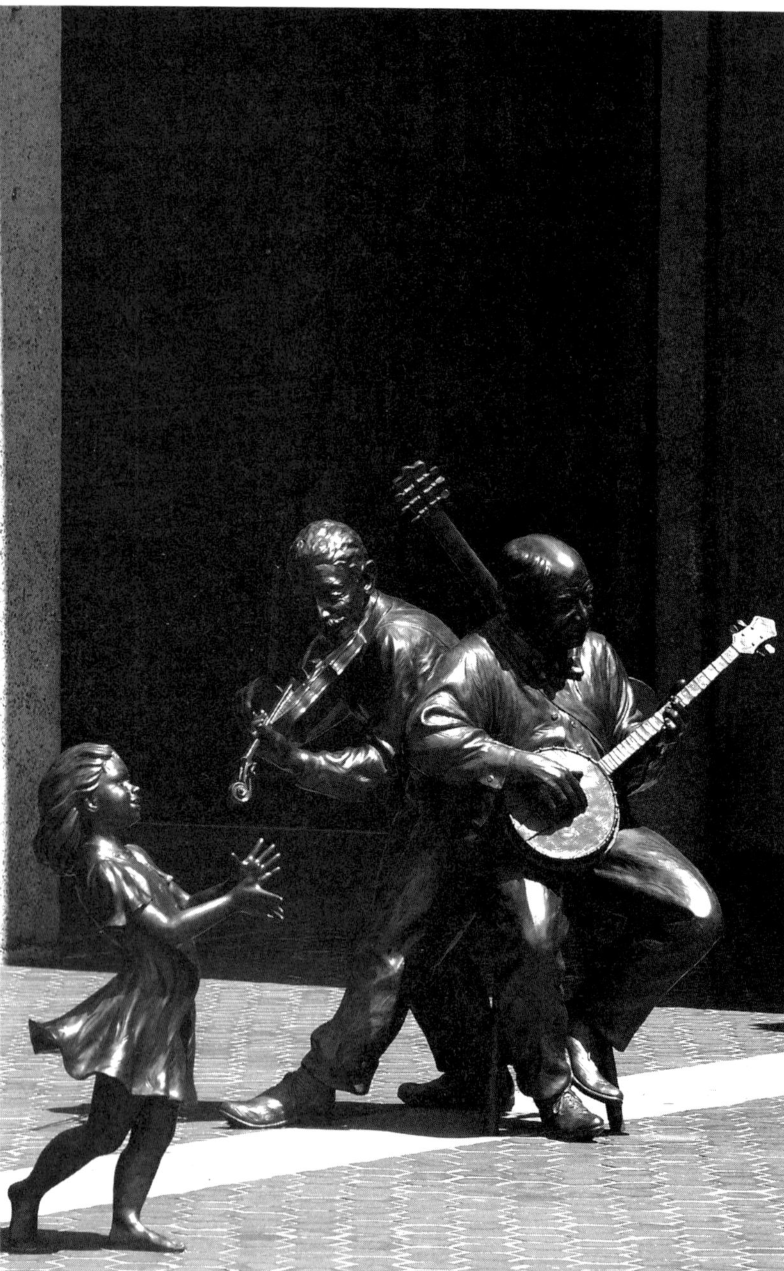

Olympus Reinvents Digital Photography

There are few people today who have yet to experience the fun and joy of digital photography—the transition from film to digital was so quick and so complete that it took many people (even those who make the cameras) by surprise. According to the research firm IDG, more than 105 million digital cameras were sold worldwide in 2006. That's a staggering number of new cameras in the hands of consumers, many of whom had never even owned a film camera that didn't have the word "disposable" printed on it.

But the majority of new cameras on the market fall into the "point-and-shoot" category, a subset of photography designed primarily to appeal to those looking to take pictures while on the move, not those looking to get the best from their photography.

The Digital SLR

To get the most from your photography it's really necessary to turn to a class of cameras known as SLRs. Short for Single Lens Reflex, SLR just refers to a type of camera where the same lens is used for viewing, focusing, and capturing your image, as opposed to the cameras often found in old movies and antique stores that used one lens for focusing and the other lens for exposing the film.

Digital SLRs are increasingly becoming the camera of choice for serious photographers. This is due to their through-the-lens (TTL) viewing system and wide choice of accessories, such as interchangeable lenses and sophisticated flash units. Photo ©Kevin Kopp

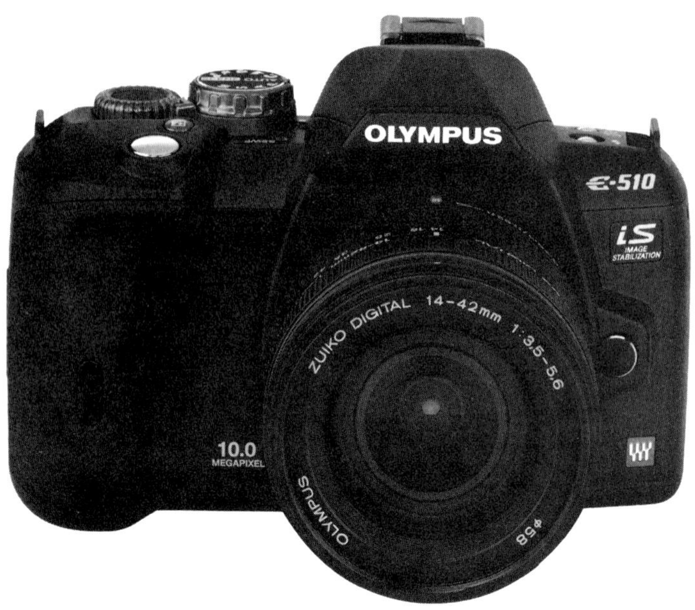

The E-510 is a highly innovative camera thanks to features such as the sensor-shift image stabilizer and Live View function. Photo ©Olympus Corporation

SLRs are fast and flexible; they allow for interchangeable lenses, usually include advanced auto-focus and auto-metering systems and generally create better images than compact or point-and-shoot cameras. That's because compact cameras are designed to favor their small size at the expense of image quality. The larger bodies of SLR cameras allow designers to put in more powerful (and therefore larger) chips, and the optics used in SLR lenses can be much more powerful. (To think of it a different way, imagine the difference in image quality between looking through a cheap drugstore magnifying glass or a laboratory quality microscope.)

But digital SLRs aren't perfect, partially because most of them are based on older film cameras. It was simply easier for most companies to modify their existing film camera designs to become the starting point for their digital models than to start from scratch. There are some important differences between the way a frame of film and a digital sensor perform though, and as a result many SLR cameras on the market have some issues with their new digital versions.

For starters, lenses designed for film (and the majority of the lenses on the market were designed during the film era) don't perform as well with digital sensors, especially at the edges of the frame. This can create big problems, especially with wide-angle shots.

Another headache found in the film-to-digital conversion is with the idea of a "focal length multiplier," a conversion needed to figure out what view the lens will provide on a digital camera. In a film camera the width of the opening at the back of the lens is the same width as the piece of film, but since a digital sensor is (usually) smaller than a piece of film, the opening ends up being larger than the sensor. This has the same effect as when you take a pair of glasses and move them away from your face while looking through them—the objects appear to be magnified.

The amount of this magnification is called the focal length multiplier and is expressed in a power (just like a telescope has a power) usually in the ranges of 1.3x to 1.6x. In order to figure out the "effective" focal length of a film lens on a digital camera, it's necessary to multiply the focal length by this number. For example on a system with a 1.5x focal length multiplier a 35mm lens will have the equivalent length of 52.5. In addition to being confusing, this makes it difficult to take wide angle photos as every lens becomes "longer" just by putting it on a digital camera.

Starting Again with "Four Thirds"

The designers at Olympus quickly realized that digital photography had a different set of challenges than film, and that by adapting film camera systems to work in a digital world companies were shackling themselves to a set of legacy problems. Why, they reasoned, would you want to lose image quality at the edges of a frame if you can design a system that avoids that?

In 2003 Olympus turned the digital photography world on its ear with a new system the company called 4/3 (pronounced "four-thirds.") This sensor has a 4:3 aspect ratio.

Instead of tying digital camera design to previous film cameras, Olympus started from scratch, creating a system that includes small, lightweight cameras and compact but incredibly sharp lenses. Each component was designed specifically for digital, so each could excel at its individual task.

Additionally, Olympus made the system "open" by publishing the specification for the lens mounts, flash-mount and other components, allowing other companies to design and produce 4/3-compatible equipment.

The first camera in Olympus's new lineup was the E-1, a professional camera that was long the flagship in the lineup. Increased interest in "prosumer" (a customer that wants a professional result without spending as much money as the pros do) cameras allowed Olympus to design a series of consumer-minded Evolt cameras, such as the latest Evolt E-510. (For simplicity sake we'll refer to the camera simply as the E-510 in the rest of this guide.)

The E-510 is the latest and greatest Olympus prosumer SLR. It boasts a ten megapixel sensor, built in dust reduction technology, image stabilization and a Live View LCD for compact-camera-like focusing and composition on a SLR camera. But to really understand what makes the E-510 so great, it's important to understand the key benefits to digital and how they differ from film photography.

Key Digital Benefits and Pitfalls

At the most simple level, digital cameras and film cameras aren't all that different; in fact the core technology of a camera hasn't changed at all in the entire history of photography. All cameras capture images by passing light through a lens aperture that is opened for a set period of time, and recording that light onto some medium. Film cameras (and their glass-plate predecessors) recorded images by creating a chemical reaction on a surface, a reaction that was later set in stone via a second chemical process.

Digital cameras record light via a series of light-sensitive dots spread in lines across the surface of a sensor. Each dot (called a pixel) records the light that falls onto it and the resolution of the sensor (and therefore the camera) is measured in megapixel, which is simply the number of pixels across horizontally multiplied by the number of pixels vertically.

Like with film, these recorded levels of light become a photograph when they're converted into numerical values by the camera and then put together to form an image. Luckily, this process happens instantly and so it's possible to get instantaneous feedback from either a raw or JPEG image (more on that in a moment) captured by your camera. This powerful instantaneous review possibility lies at the heart of what makes digital photography so popular. It's no longer necessary to wait hours or days to see the results of one's photography.

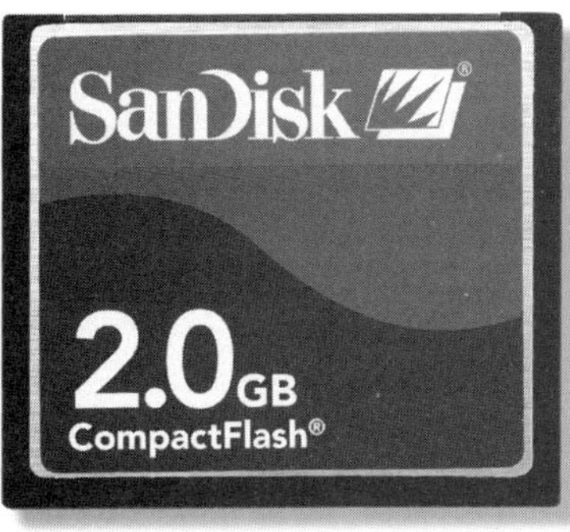

One advantage of shooting digital is there is no film to buy. Memory cards such as this 2.0 GB CompactFlash card can be used over and over again in the Evolt E-510 camera. Photo ©SanDisk Corporation

In Search of ISO

The chemicals that record light in film photography are sensitive to light, but they can be made more sensitive to light by changing their chemical composition. The higher the ISO number, the more sensitive the film would be to light, meaning less light would be needed to create the same image. Each time the ISO doubles, the sensitivity to light doubles, so that ISO 100 film is half as sensitive to light as ISO 200 film. This allowed different films to work in different levels of light, but it also required that the photographer change rolls of film as lighting conditions changed.

Digital sensors don't have a fixed ISO sensitivity, in order to make the sensor more reactive to light it is necessary to boost the electrical charge going into the chip. A simple change of the ISO setting on the camera can raise or lower its sensitivity. Like with film a doubling of the ISO level doubles the sensitivity. Unlike with film where ISO was set by the roll, ISO on digital cameras can be set per-image and changed at any time.

Generally speaking the more sensitive the setting, the more "noise" that will be produced. Similar to the grain seen in film, noise is the result of the increased electrical charge running through the sensor (while grain was the chemical reaction to light causing clumping). While it's possible to capture low-light pictures at ISO 1600 on most digital cameras, they'll often be rife with annoying splotches of color noise.

Stabilize Your Shot

This is one of the reasons that many companies are turning to image stabilization, a method of compensating for camera motion via gyroscopes built into either the camera or the lens, allowing photographers to handhold a shot in lowlight where otherwise they'd have to go to a higher (noisier) ISO setting. The Olympus E-510 has built-in Image Stabilization features, allowing for more creative control (more on this in the next chapter).

Watch What You Shoot

One of the key advances of digital photography is the instantaneous review of images on the rear-mounted LCD screen. This screen is used for more than just image-review though, as digital cameras offer a wealth of menus, custom settings and more available through the rear LCD screen.

Additionally the E-510 provides a feature called Live-View LCD that allows you to focus and compose your images on the rear LCD instead of through the viewfinder (more on this in the next chapter as well).

Balance Your Light

The human eye performs a neat trick, one that evolved over millions of years. Our brains are able to adjust to the color of the light we see and we automatically balance that color out. A piece of paper appears equally white to us whether we're looking at it under a bank of fluorescent lights or bright sunlight. But in each case the color of white is slightly different. That's why daylight balanced film that was shot under fluorescent lights (think an office cubicle) comes out looking sickly green.

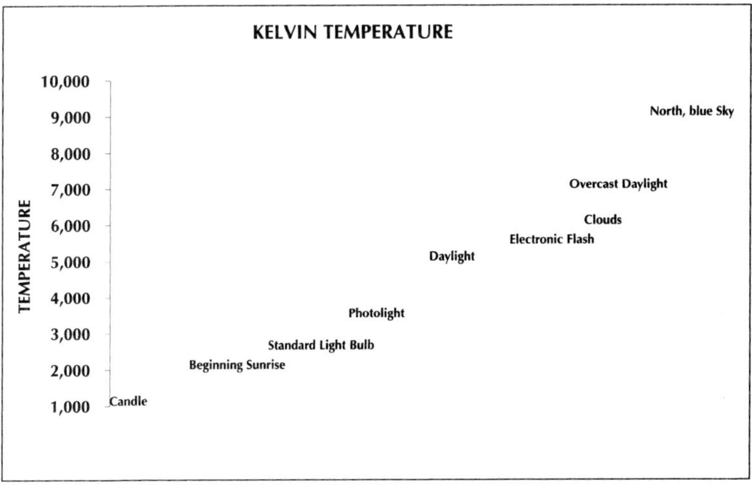

Approximate K temperature of common light sources.

The "color" of white is measured using a scale called Kelvin, and each color has a different "temperature" on that scale going from slightly red to slightly blue in hue.

With film it was necessary to match not only the ISO of the film to the lighting condition but also to pair the right light with the right film emulsion. If you were stuck with the wrong type of film in your camera you either had to waste the end of the roll and switch films, or put a filter over your lens to convert the incoming light to the right color temperature for the film. What a headache.

Digital sensors function more like our eyes, and can be adjusted to match the lighting condition at hand, shot after shot. Even better, if you're shooting raw you can make this adjustment after you take your image, even correcting for situations when you've left the camera on the wrong setting.

To Shoot Raw or Not to Shoot Raw—That is the Question

Looking back at the description of how a digital sensor works, we see that a digital camera is really just recording a string of numbers corresponding to the level of light at each pixel. To simplify things, we'll say that each pixel can produce a value for the red, green, and blue light striking it. (This is not exactly true, but the actual function of a digital sensor is convoluted and not terribly important at this point.) All colors we see can be described in terms of the combination of red, green, and blue light. As light strikes the pixels it causes a change in electrical resistance at the pixel, which results in a numerical value, which is represented between 0 and 255. (Again, this is a simplification for instructional purposes.) A nice deep purple might have a red value of 122, a green value of 15, and a blue value of 178.

For photos that need to be processed quickly and/or submitted via email, JPEG is an excellent format choice. Photo ©M. Morgan

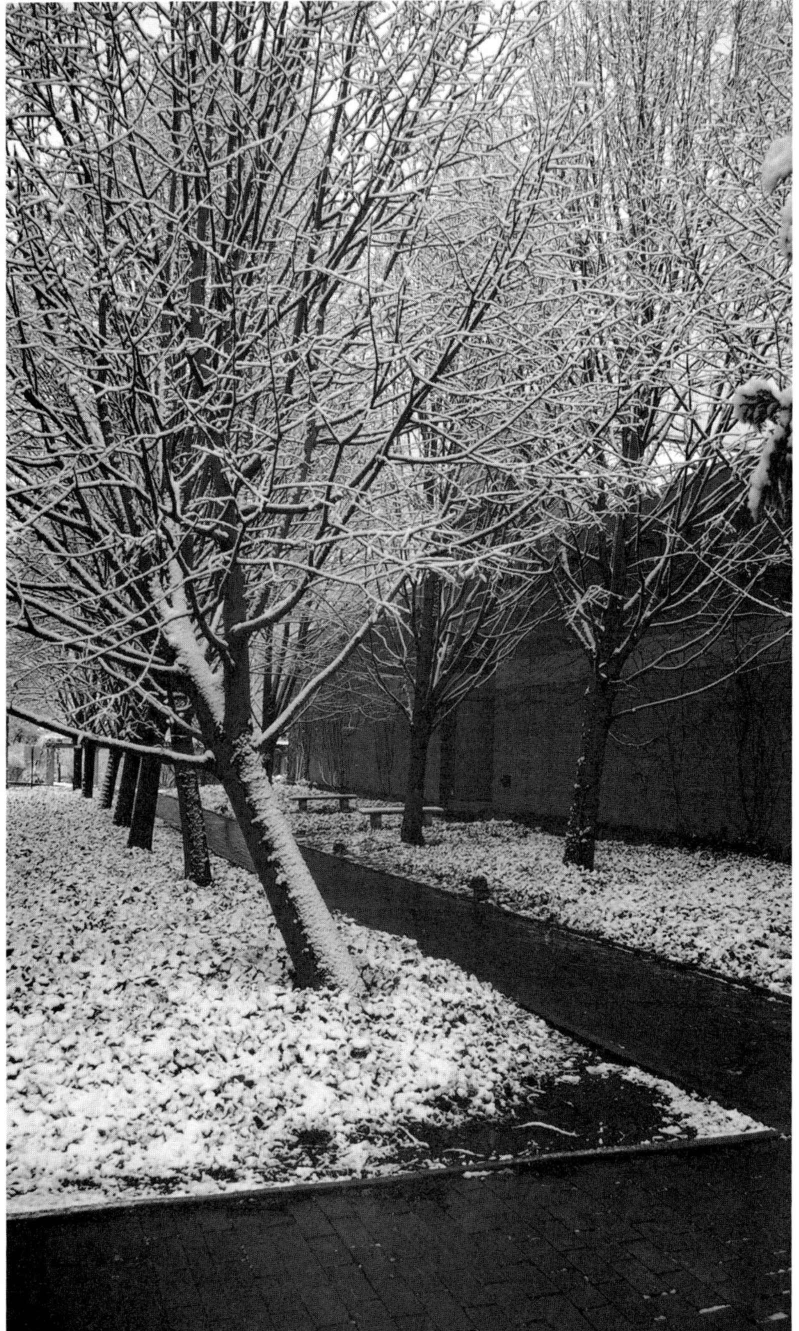

Most digital cameras can record this data in two different formats—raw or JPEG. A raw file is simply a representation of all of the information that comes off the sensor, essentially a string of numbers with no evaluation made as how those would look as real colors. A raw file, like a negative, needs to be processed by your computer in order to see the picture.

A JPEG meanwhile is created in-camera from the data off of the sensor, and is a much smaller file. It would seem like JPEG was the better format to use, since you don't have to do anything to the file after capturing it, but that's not really the case.

While the raw file needs a program to convert the file into an image, the format contains significantly more information that a JPEG. Designed to be as compact as possible, the JPEG file throws away information it thinks you wont need. That's fine if you perfectly expose your photos every single time, but if you don't (and really, no one does) having a raw file to edit later on can be a big help. It'll allow you to fix things like under or overexposed images, incorrect white balances, and more.

For example, if you shoot an image while your camera's white balance setting is set to cloudy and you're really under fluorescent lights you're going to get a picture with a really ugly color cast. But if you've shot that in raw you can simply dial in the right white balance in your software and fix it, without causing any problems with the rest of your image. With a JPEG you might be able to fix the color cast, but you're just as likely to throw off the color of someone's face or their clothes in the process.

Many people shoot in a mode called raw+JPEG, where the camera creates both a raw file and a JPEG file each time you press the shutter release button. This a good mode for shooters not yet familiar with the software needed for raw editing but who might want to go back at some point and change their files, but it creates two files for each shot. Not a big deal in this age of larger memory cards and super-large, super-cheap hard drives, but it's something to keep in mind.

Incidentally, you might be wondering how you can review an image taken in raw mode on the LCD if raw files require post-processing to be viewable. Each camera with a raw mode records a very small JPEG preview into the raw file, just big enough to display well on your LCD screen in order to help with composition and shooting. But you'll get much more control over the image when you edit it on your computer.

The Digital Advantage

There are so many reasons to shoot digital that it's no wonder that the market has exploded over the last few years. Digital SLR cameras like the E-510 offer unprecedented created freedom and control, with almost none of the costs or headaches associated with film photography. By mastering the controls of the E-510 you'll be able to take your photography to a higher level in no time at all.

Note: When the terms "left" and "right" or "back" and "front" are used to describe the locations of various camera controls, we assume that the camera is being held in shooting position.

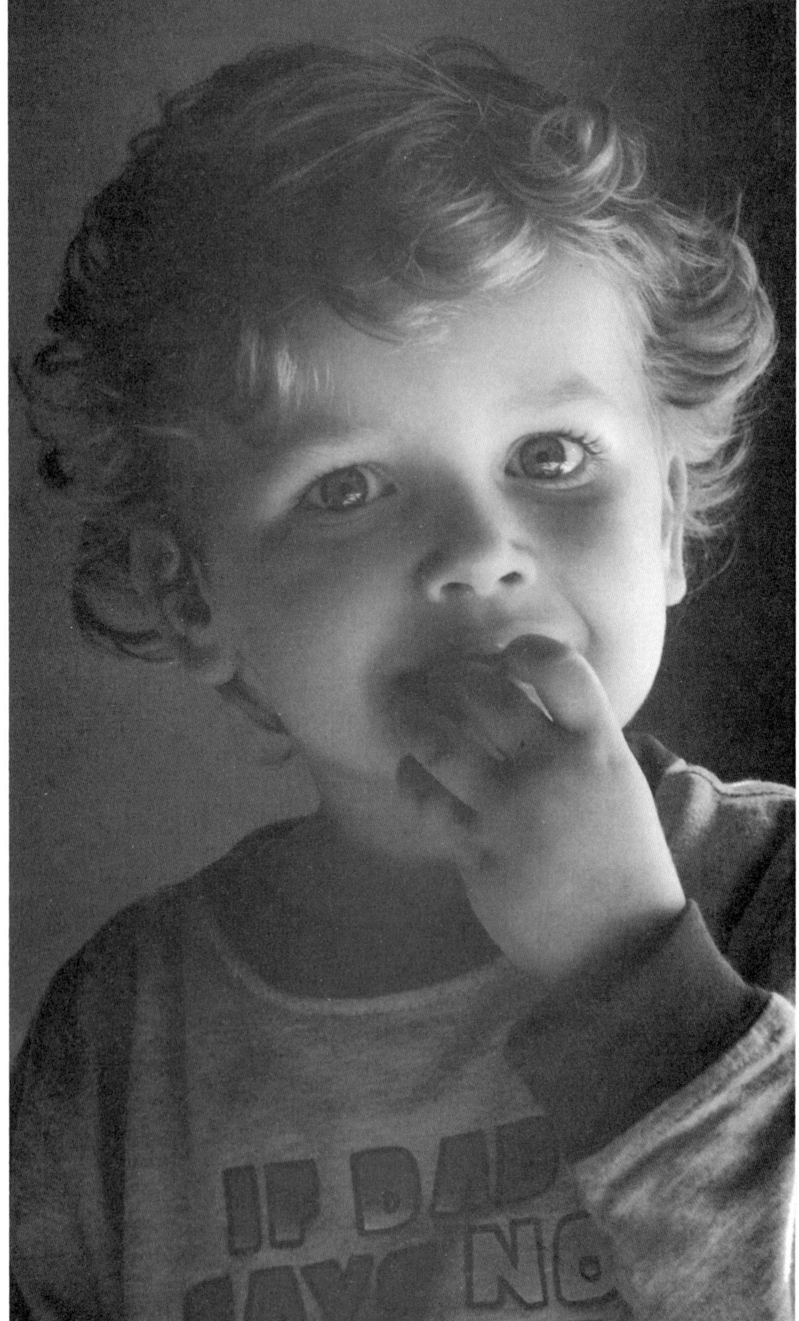
IF DAD
NO

Understanding Features and Functions

The E-510, a member of a long line of excellent Olympus digital SLRs and accessories, is from a company with a legacy of producing high-quality yet affordable cameras. The E-510 is chock-full of features, so many in fact that the average user will never get to every single custom menu option or shooting mode. Of course it's always better for a camera to have too-many features than too few, especially if those features offer a wealth of creative shooting possibilities. There's nothing wrong with growing into your camera—it's much less problematic than growing out of it.

It's important to remember too that there's no way to "waste" a picture as in the days of film. You can play with your camera's features to your heart's delight and keep only the shots that look good or have some interesting creative effect. In fact, most people become familiar with their camera primarily by trying different settings and seeing how the images look.

The E-510 is a highly evolved digital camera, utilizing state-of-the-art dust removal, image stabilization, and other technologies not even found on most professional-level cameras. While powerful, the camera was designed from the start to be compact, durable and convenient to use. The buttons, menu options and controls have been laid out across the 16.2 ounce (460 g.) body.

The Evolt E-510 offers an abundance of features and controls for creative photography, along with the ability of friends and family to use the camera for "point-and-shoot" photography in full AUTO mode. Photo ©Haley Pritchard

The E-510 is based on Olympus's 4/3 system and as such accepts virtually every lens and accessory designed by any of the 4/3 partner companies. The range of Olympus Zuiko digital lenses are compatible with the E-510 and provide sharp, colorful images without the artifacts usually associated with digital photography.

The rear 2.5 inch (6.4 cm) rear LCD is not only the information control center for the camera, but can be used in Olympus's Live View mode as a focusing tool offering onscreen magnification up to 10x life size for super-accurate image composition.

Overview of Features

- Olympus-exclusive 4/3 size 10.1 megapixel Live MOS Sensor
- Internal image stabilization system that allows for motion-free images even at low light
- 49 zone multi-pattern metering system
- Supersonic Wave Filter for automatic dust-removal
- Live View system that allows for real-time focus using the rear 2.5 inch LCD and provides magnified zoom for critical focus
- Three frames-per-second with a seven-shot raw buffer
- Twenty-eight shooting modes that include five different exposure modes and 18 scene modes
- Exposure, white balance and focus bracketing modes
- Built in pop-up flash
- Depth of field preview button
- On screen image review including shooting details and histogram.
- Dual xD and CompactFlash card slots.

Olympus E-510 – Front View

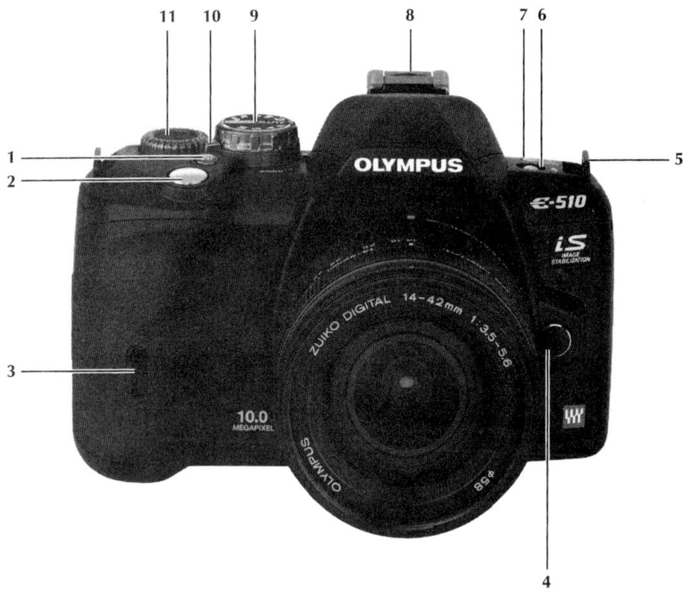

1. *Exposure compensation button*
2. *Shutter button*
3. *Self-timer/Remote control lamp/Remote control receiver*
4. *Lens release button*
5. *Strap eyelet*
6. *Flash button*
7. *Sequential shooting/ Self-timer/Remote control button; Copy/Print button*
8. *Hot shoe*
9. *Mode dial*
10. *Power switch*
11. *Control dial*

Olympus E-510 – Back View

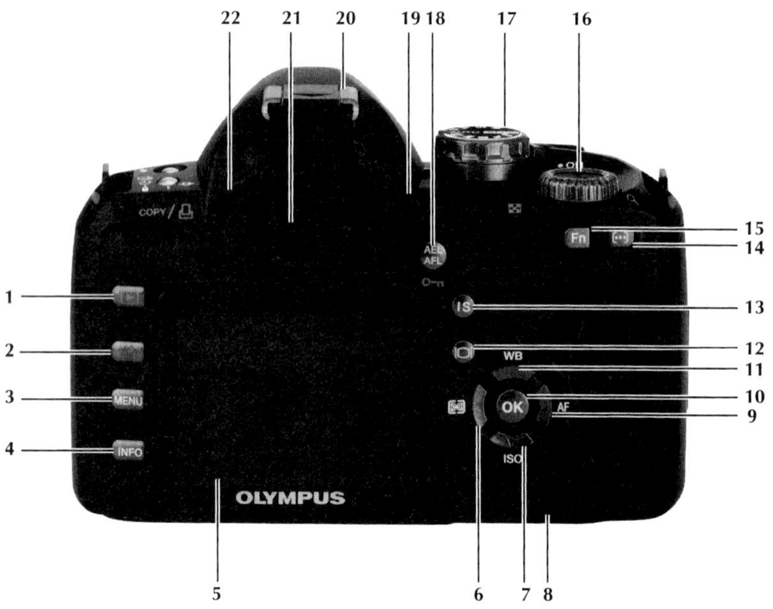

1. *Playback button*
2. *Erase button*
3. *Menu button*
4. *Information Display button*
5. *LCD monitor*
6. *Left arrow*
7. *Down arrow*
8. *USB Video out*
9. *Right arrow*
10. *OK button*
11. *Up arrow*
12. *Live view button*
13. *IS button*
14. *AF frame button*
15. *Fn button*
16. *Control dial*
17. *Mode dial*
18. *AEL/AFL button*
19. *Diopter adjustment dial*
20. *Hot shoe*
21. *Viewfinder*
22. *Eyecup*

Olympus E-510 – Top View

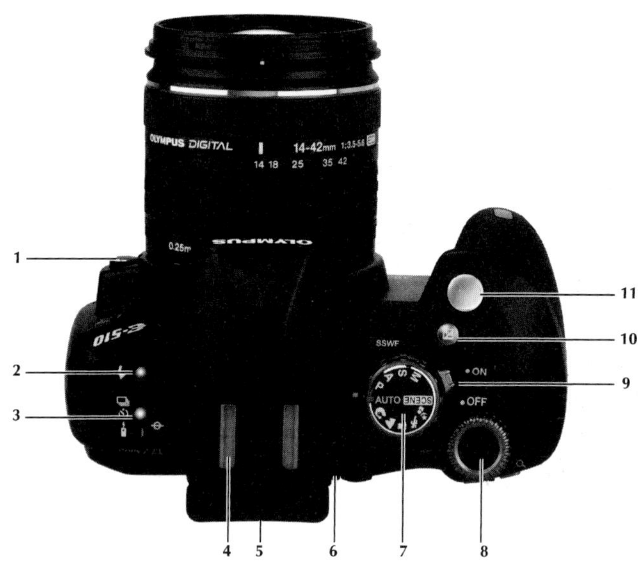

1. *Lens release button*
2. *Flash button*
3. *Sequential shooting/ Self-timer/Remote control button; Copy/Print button*
4. *Hot shoe*
5. *Viewfinder*
6. *Diopter adjustment dial*
7. *Mode dial*
8. *Control dial*
9. *Power switch*
10. *Exposure compensation button*
11. *Shutter button*

Camera Controls

Like with many of today's digital SLR cameras, the E-510 can be controlled via the Mode Dial and the Control Dial, located on the top right of the camera, and via the menus. Navigation though the menus is accomplished via the Arrow Pad. Users can control all aspects of the camera operation via a combination of these controls.

Mode Dial: Located on the top right of the camera, directly above the power switch, the mode dial is used to select the camera's main shooting modes. This dial is divided in two parts by the AUTO setting: on one side are the advanced shooting modes such as: Manual, Shutter Priority, Aperture Priority, and Program, while the easy shooting modes (Portrait, Landscape, Macro, Sports, and Night) occupy the other half of the control.

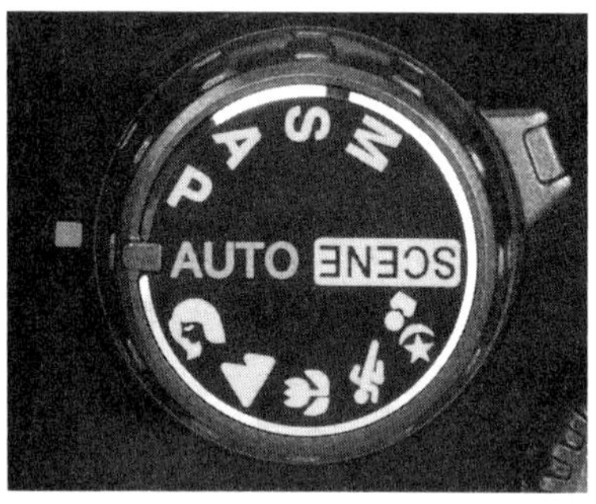

Control Dial: Located just behind and to the right of the Mode Dial, the Control dial allows the user to set various functions quickly. Usually operated by the thumb while the camera is in

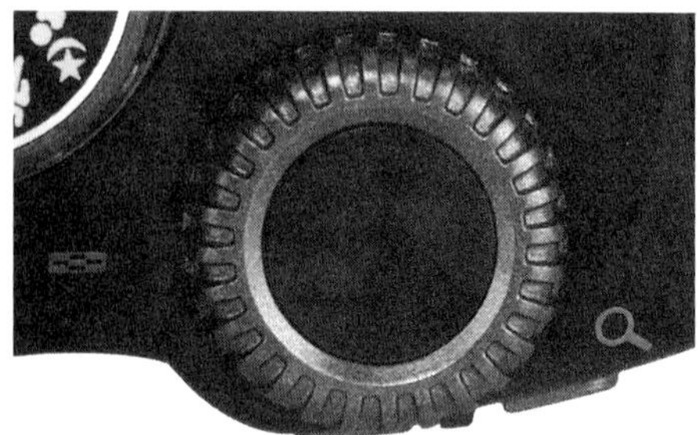

shooting position, the Control dial quickly makes settings such as aperture and shutter speed. The function of this dial depends on the shooting mode selected on the Mode dial. Some modes do not take advantage of this dial.

Shutter Button: As with most modern cameras, the shutter release on the E-510 is a two-stage trigger, pressing the release halfway activates the autoexposure and autofocus settings (when enabled). Pressing the shutter release all the way triggers the shutter and captures an image.

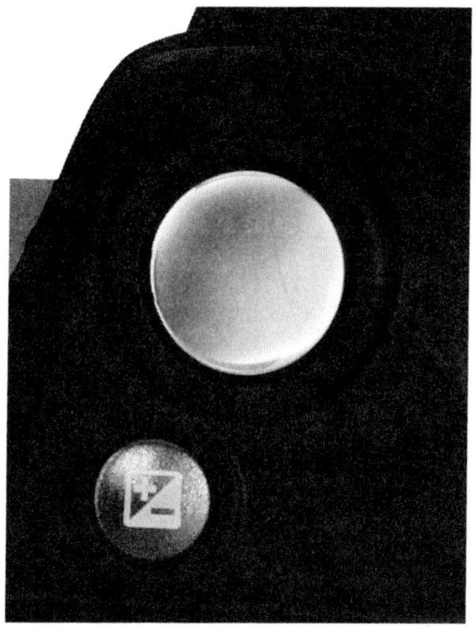

Arrow Keys: The four keys on the rear of the E-510, to the right of the LCD display are used to navigate the menu choices and make selections using the OK button. Additionally, the four Arrow Keys are used as buttons to make quick selections while shooting. Clockwise starting at the top they provide access to white balance **WB** , autofocus **AF** , ISO **ISO** and metering modes . By pressing these keys while the camera is on, it's possible to jump directly to the controls for those camera features. Once the appropriate quick access screen is up, the Control dial or the arrow keys can be used to move between

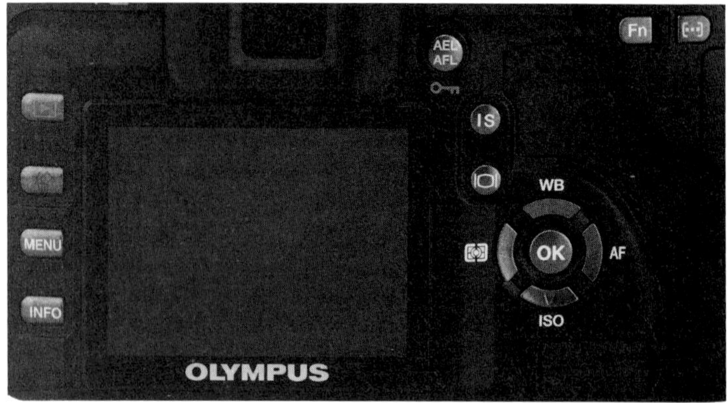

The menu button, located to the left of the LCD monitor, is used to access the E-510's main menu display.

settings. Either press the center OK button (OK) or half-press the shutter release

Menus Overview

The Olympus E-510 has two distinct menu modes. Once the shutter is pressed halfway, the rear LCD panel displays information to augment the internal viewfinder informational display. This menu mode doesn't provide access to the key features, but shows all the camera's current settings. Pressing the Info button **INFO** toggles between the detailed and the basic display modes.

Pressing the Menu button **MENU** brings up the E-510 main menu display. This is broken into five sections, displayed down the left side of the LCD screen. The first two are camera settings for adjustment of the shooting modes. 1 2 The third is for setting the playback features ▶ . The remaining two are for controlling camera settings and defaults such as file quality and date/time settings. 1 2

You can think of the menu on the E-510 as if it were made up of three columns. Pressing the Menu button brings up the main display. Using the up or down arrow keys moves up and down the first column, which are the main functions. Pressing the right key moves the focus to the second column, where you can once again move up and down the rows in that column to select camera functions you'd like to modify. When you have highlighted the menu item you want to change (you'll know because the choice will display in yellow) you can then move to the final column—the one with the various settings for that function. Pressing either the OK button or half-pressing the shutter release will make your selection. You can cancel at any time before making a selection by hitting the Menu button again.

Camera Activation

Powering The Camera

The E-510 is powered by a high-powered Lithium-Ion rechargeable battery rated at 1500 mAh. The high capacity battery pack is capable of taking several hundred shots under the right circumstances. Features like Live View will drain the battery more quickly, as will consistent use of the LCD for image review. Additionally, the built-in strobe takes its toll on battery life as well, which is one of the reasons that pro photographers usually rely on external flash systems.

Also keep in mind that the camera utilizes power from the battery any time the E-510 is connected to a PC via the built-in USB 2.0 port, so turning off the camera after image transfer or using an external card reader will lengthen battery life.

The E-510 comes with a charger that will replenish the battery in around two hours, and the charger can handle voltages between 100v and 240v, making it suitable for international use with the right adapter cord.

Power Switch

The power switch on the E-510 is located on the top right of the camera, directly next to the viewfinder and integrated into the Mode dial.

Auto Power Off

Like other digital cameras, the E-510 will enter a sleep mode after a power of inactivity to conserve battery life. Pressing the shutter release halfway will wake the camera from sleep if it's been idle for a short period of time, however if its left to idle too long, the camera will need to be turned off and on again to wake from sleep.

Saving battery life is great, but often times you'll find that the camera's default one-minute sleep time is too short. When photographing many subjects, especially active ones, if your camera goes into sleep mode it can delay the amount of time it takes to lock onto your subject and capture a photo.

Luckily, you can change the sleep time via the camera's menu choices. Press the Menu button on the left side of the LCD display on the back of the camera. Press the down arrow until the second settings menu is displayed . Press the right arrow to move to the second column and then press the down arrow until <SLEEP> is highlighted. Now press the right arrow again and select a setting from <OFF> to <10 MIN> with the up and down arrow. When you've got the setting you'd prefer, press the OK button or half-press the shutter release.

Remember, this is a tradeoff. A longer sleep setting will keep the camera active and using the battery longer but will leave the camera ready to shoot at a moment's notice.

Date and Time

When the E-510 is first turned on it will automatically remind the user to set the date and the time with a large red icon of a clock with YMD displayed under it. Many image management programs use the date and time data that's writ-

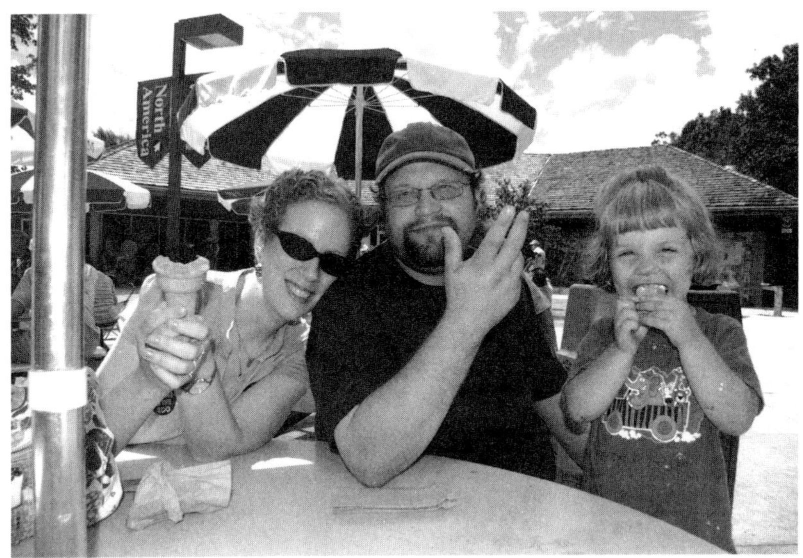

The E-510 sleep mode is designed to save battery life. However, the default time of one minute means the camera will almost always be asleep, causing the camera not to fire immediately when desired. You can lengthen the time so that the camera is ready to shoot except during long periods of inactivity. Photo ©M. Morgan

ten to each photo in order to help organize image collections, so it's important to set this.

This setting is the first choice under the second setup menu. 2 Press the Menu button and scroll down the column with the down arrow button until you come to the setup icon. Press the right arrow button and move to the second column, and the first option will be <YMD>. Press the right arrow again and use the arrow keys to enter the current time and date.

The Viewfinder

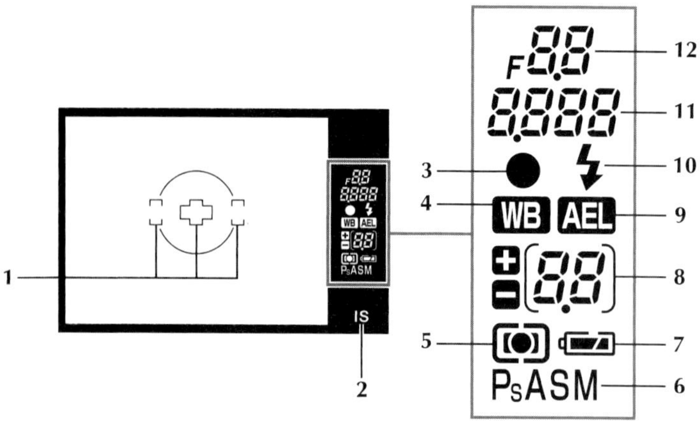

1. *AF frame*
2. *Image stabilizer*
3. *AF confirmation mark*
4. *White balance*
5. *Metering mode*
6. *Exposure mode*
7. *Battery check*
8. *Exposure compensation value*
9. *AE lock*
10. *Flash*
11. *Shutter speed*
12. *Aperture value*

The Olympus E-510 uses a standard eye-level single-lens-reflex viewfinder with a quick return half-mirror, but also offers a unique Live View mode via the LCD (see page 41). A manual diopter dial on the right side of the viewfinder eyepiece allows for optical corrections for those who wish to adjust the camera to match their eyeglass prescriptions. Simply look through the viewfinder and turn the diopter adjustment until the AF lines on the viewing screen are as sharp as possible.

The camera's diopter adjustment isn't very wide-ranging though, it only provides a slight correction so it's not really enough for people with even moderate prescriptions. Best is probably to continue to shoot with glasses, using the diopter adjustment for the slight distortion that creates.

The viewfinder offers a 95% field of view, meaning that the camera is actually capturing about 5% more of the scene in front of you than you'll see through the viewfinder. This is better than many other SLR cameras in this class, which have a much lower percentage of coverage.

The fixed-type focusing screen is not interchangeable though it is possible to display ruled lines in the viewfinder in the Live View mode (see below). The E-510's viewfinder provides shooting information such as selected aperture, shutter speed, and more.

LCD Monitor

The E-510 has a particularly useful LCD display because it's used not only for the selection of menu items but is also used in the Live View mode to view and compose images. The high-resolution 2.5 inch (6.4 cm) display has 230,000 pixels and offers 100% coverage of the image when used in Live View mode.

The LCD screen has several brightness settings, though they're a bit hard to find if you don't know where to look. Press the Menu button and, using the arrow key, navigate down to the second settings menu 2 and then use the right arrow to move over to the second column. Scroll down until you reach the brightness setting, which looks like a screen with a series of small vertical lines under it. . It's possible to set the LCD screen to any of 14 brightness levels using the right and left arrow keys and the OK button.

The LCD screen can also be used for image evaluation after capture, and it can provide a wealth of information on your photograph, though it can't be used during the brief playback of the most-recently captured image. It's possible to view an image's histogram, overexposure points and more.

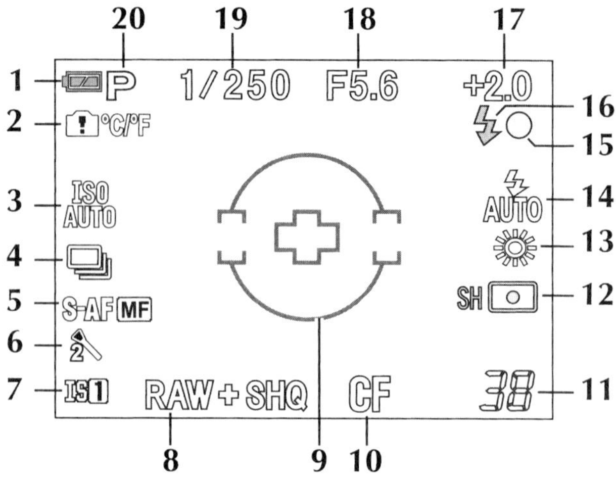

1. *Battery check*
2. *Internal temperature warning*
3. *ISO*
4. *Sequential shooting*
5. *AF mode*
6. *Picture mode*
7. *Image stabilizer*
8. *Record mode*
9. *AF frame*
10. *Card*
11. *Number of storable still pictures*
12. *Metering mode*
13. *White balance*
14. *Flash mode*
15. *AF confirmation mark*
16. *Flash*
17. *Exposure compensation value*
18. *Aperture value*
19. *Shutter speed*
20. *Exposure mode*

After you capture an image, wait until the review image has gone away, or if you prefer you can change this time by hitting the Menu button, scrolling down with the arrow key to the second Setup screen 2 and then hitting the right arrow to move to the second column until you come to <Rec View>. Press the right arrow button and move to the third column to select how long the camera should display the review image. It's possible to select a time range from <OFF> to <20 SEC>. The up arrow key will increase the time of the review playback and the down arrow key will decrease it.

Press the green Play button located on the top left of the back panel of the camera, just to the left of the LCD display to bring up your image and then press the Info button. The first time you press the button the camera will display the storage media used (either xD or CF), the file format (RAW or JPEG—including the JPEG compression—or both) the file name and the sequence number of the shot.

The next press of the Info button calls up the size (in pixels) of the image and the compression settings of the JPEG file. Pressing the Info button another time brings up the histogram display, showing the recorded information in each of the red, green, and blue channels, as well as showing the combined histogram. This mode also shows complete shooting information including the white balance and color modes. Yet another press brings up a larger histogram mode, filling the image with a single histogram displaying information for each channel combined.

Moving away from histograms for a moment, pressing the button again toggles in to a highlight warning mode, where overexposed parts of the image blink to show problem areas where detail is lost in the highlight, and a final press of the button shifts to a shadow warning mode, where the screen blinks in areas that are underexposed.

The camera can be left in any of these modes so that subsequent images are in the same review mode as the previous shot. The combination of different evaluative modes is very handy for the photographer looking for the utmost in their images.

The camera will also automatically rotate images on playback so that vertical shots turn 90° to fill the viewfinder. If you prefer to leave this in the standard cropped mode, simply press the Menu button and arrow-down until you get to the <Play> menu and select the rotate choice . Select <OFF> to disable this feature.

The Control dial is particularly useful during image review. By default the camera is in 100% view, where playback of an image is not zoomed in. By turning the Control dial counter-clockwise it's possible to zoom into the image up to 14x the original size. This is useful for checking focus and the level of detail. While in this zoom mode, the arrow buttons ◁ ▷ △ ▽ control panning around the image.

Turning the Control dial clockwise from the default position, though, moves into the thumbnail display, providing between four and twenty previews depending on the selected setting. A final clockwise turn of the dial puts the E-510 into a unique calendar view, where it's possible to inspect images on a CF or xD card based on the date they were shot, using the arrow keys to move between the days and the OK button to select the date.

The delete button 🗑 next to the LCD screen is used to delete images, either directly after capture during their immediate playback, or when reviewing images after shooting. Pressing the button will result in a confirmation screen (unless a custom setting to eliminate the warning is enabled, see page 78) and a press of the OK button will delete the image.

Scene Modes

The LCD screen is also used to choose between the E-510's preset Scene modes. Turning the Main dial to the Scene SCENE setting switches the LCD to the scene selection mode. Pressing the up and down arrows on the Arrow pad toggles between the different shooting modes such as landscape, beach, and panorama. Each mode preset includes a brief description of the function.

As a quick tip, once you've set a scene, the camera sticks to that mode as long as the Main dial is set to Scene. In order to select a new scene, either move the dial to one of the five presets on the Control dial or rotate the dial away from Scene and then back to Scene any time the camera is "awake."

Live View

Unique among prosumer digital SLRs is Olympus's inclusion of a Live View function in the E-510, which turns the LCD viewfinder into a compositional viewfinder.

Simply press the Live View button |O| on the rear of the camera to the right of the viewfinder while the camera is awake to switch it into Live View mode. The mirror will flip up and the LCD menu system will be replaced with a live preview of the scene you're about to shoot.

Pressing the Info button in the Live View mode it's possible to toggle again through different informational views, including shooting information, histogram and compositional grid. To activate the grid, start by pressing Menu, scrolling to the first setup menu 2 , pressing the right arrow to move to second column and selecting Frame Assist and then pressing the right arrow to move to the third column and selecting Golden Section, Grid or Scale.

Once the shot is composed, fully press the shutter-release button. The mirror will flip down and then up again briefly as the camera focuses and meters the shot, and the camera will capture your image.

There are a few considerations when using Live View. One is that it shortens the life of the battery. Another is that it takes longer to capture the image. Finally, another important consideration when capturing images using Live View is the relative noise of your images. Using the feature "over a long period" (according to Olympus) causes images shot with high ISOs to exhibit especially noisy artifacts because of heat buildup on the sensor. It's recommended that Live View be used with low ISO images, and the feature can be disengaged for a while to let the sensor cool down.

Image Sensor

The E-510 features Olympus's 10.0 effective megapixel sensor with 3648 x 2736 pixels on the 17.3 x 13.0 mm sensor. Olympus has spent a considerable amount of time designing a sensor that complements the small form and light weight of the E-510 yet provides low noise and high image quality.

The sensor in the E-510 provides a very high-quality image, and in fact is the highest resolution sensor currently in Olympus's arsenal.

Olympus utilizes their 4/3 format/lens system. As a result, the company's 7-14mm lens has the equivalent of a 14-28mm lens in 35mm format. We will use the actual focal length, however, when discussing lenses in this text.

The sensor (for those who want to get really technical) uses a standard Bayer pattern RGB filter, which features more green sensitive pixels than red or blue, to match the sensitivity of the human eye. The camera also utilizes a fixed low-pass anti-aliasing filter in order to prevent image distortions and color artifacts.

Anti-Shock

Instead of a traditional mirror lockup (whereby the mirror is locked into place on the first shutter press and released on a second, and the shutter is operated independently) to reduce blur on long-exposure shots, the E-510 uses an anti-shake system that provides a fixed interval after mirror lockup before the shutter is triggered. This is particularly helpful in astrophotography or macro photography where camera-shake is a large problem. To set the Anti-Shock feature press the Menu button and then scroll down to the second shooting menu 2 and then use the right arrow to move to the second column. Select <Anti-Shock> and then use the right arrow to move to the third column to select the interval, from <1SEC> – <30SEC>.

Image Stabilization

The E-510 uses an advanced internal Image Stabilization system to prevent the motion blur often associated with shooting low-speed images, especially with long lenses. Internal gyroscopes react to physical motion and then internal motors move the imaging sensor to compensate for this movement. Since the system is built into the camera, it's not necessary to purchase specific image stabilization lenses.

To engage the image stabilization function simply press the IS button on the rear of the camera, which brings up an <IMAGE STABILIZATION> menu with three choices.

<OFF> disables the image stabilization system (but pressing and holding the IS button acts as a shortcut for turning it back on. An IS1 icon IS1 will illuminate in the bottom right of the viewfinder. <I.S. 1> turns on the stabilization for horizontal images, while <I.S. 2> turns it on for vertically composed photos.

Neither mode will counteract the effects of excessive shake and very slow speeds, so it's best to use a tripod in either of these situations.

Memory Cards

The E-510 is unique in that it accepts both the Olympus-designed xD cards found in the company's compact digital lineup and the more standard (for SLR photography) CompactFlash cards.

Both xD and CF cards are relatively durable, but they don't like to be exposed to heat or water, so keep them out of damp and hot locations.

CF cards are available in enormous capacities, which is good because the 10 megapixel sensor in the E-510 creates large files. (See page 54 for specifics).

It's important to make sure that the camera isn't writing to either the xD or the CF cards while they are being removed from the camera. This can damage the contents of the cards and damage your images. A red LED on the right of the rear panel near the memory card door will illuminate while the camera is writing data to the cards. Wait until this light is off before removing cards. (Better yet, turn off the camera when removing a card and wait until the light goes off.)

To insert a card simply open the memory door on the right side of the camera. xD cards are spring loaded and you'll just need to press it into place until it "catches." CF cards need to insert completely into the slot. Both cards can only insert in one direction, so don't force the cards.

Close the memory card bay door, power on the camera and begin shooting. When you're ready to remove the card, open the door again. For xD cards simply press them in completely again, this will release the catch holding them in place. CF cards are ejected by pressing on the small ejection button underneath the slot.

It's possible to change the naming scheme used by the camera by going to the second setup menu 2 and selecting <EDIT FILENAME> from the second column of choices. Using the arrow buttons you can use the up and down arrow keys to change the first two letters of the file name, using the right arrow to move between the first and second characters.

By selecting Menu then the second setup menu 2 you can reset the sequential file number counter.

Formatting Your Memory Card

In order to use a memory card with the E-510 it's necessary to format it. Every camera system uses a different file structure, and formatting guarantees that the card is set up to work with the E-510. Formatting will erase all of the images on the card, so be sure to transfer any important photos or files to your computer before formatting.

To format your card simply hit Menu and select the first shooting menu and then use the right arrow to move to the second column and select <CARD SETUP>. Use the arrows to select <FORMAT> and then use the arrows again to select <YES> and press the enter key. It's essential to reformat your card periodically to keep it functioning properly.

Cleaning Your Camera

A clean camera is a dust-free camera, so be sure to keep your camera neat and free of dust, oils, and any other residue that can affect image quality of the condition of your gear. It's best to keep fluids away from the camera as they can only serve to damage the sensitive electrical insides, but a dry cloth should be more than enough to clean the outside of the camera.

The inside of the camera body can be carefully cleaned with a photographic bulb-syringe and the lens elements can be cleaned with a lens-cloth.

Sensor Cleaning

The bane of the digital photographer's existence is sensor dust, tiny specs of material that get onto the imaging sensor and cling there, showing up as dark spots in frame after frame.

The E-510 combats this with a built-in dust removal tool called Supersonic Wave that uses a transparent filter in front of the lens as a sort of windshield to protect against dust. By shaking this filter rapidly the dust falls off, and doesn't end up in the frame. The E-510 performs this when powered on, so there's no need to mess with menu settings to activate this feature.

A <CLEANING MODE> option under the second setup menu 2 will lock the mirror up and open the shutter without triggering the sensor to activate. This is important because the charge of the sensor attracts dust. By activating this mode it's possible to clean off the sensor using a light puff of air from a blower, just be sure to never ever touch the tip of the blower to the sensor, and to never use a chemical product like compressed air. We have to advise that you do this with extreme care and at your own risk. If, despite all, the sensor has dirt on it that won't come off with the methods described above, take your camera to an authorized service center for professional cleaning.

Getting Started in Seven Easy Steps

In order to start shooting with the E-510 as quickly as possible there are a few key settings to check. Following this guide will get you up and shooting as quickly as possible.

1. **Set your date and time:** You'll want to be sure that your images have the right time stamps on them, so set this feature as soon as your get your camera.

2. Set the auto-power-off time to something longer than the default one minute. You can always turn your camera off if you're going to leave it for several minutes unattended, so setting this feature to something more useful (maybe five minutes) will be helpful.

3. **Change your image quality settings:** At very least you should record a high-resolution (SHQ) image, but if you plan to get serious about your photography and take advantage of all that the E-510 has to offer, then set it to shoot raw + JPEG. (See page 52)

4. **Set your shooting mode:** If you're just getting started with your camera, try Auto mode on the Main dial, which will pick all the settings for you. As you get more familiar with the camera, try out aperture priority, shutter priority or even manual mode.

   Alternately you can try one of the preset scenes, set via the Main dial's default scene positions, or by putting the dial in the Scene setting and using the menu to select the appropriate scene.

5. **Set your autofocus mode:** Set your focus area to Auto by pressing the Autofocus button, located on the top right of the camera [▪▪▪] and then selecting Auto.

6. **Set your drive mode:** Press the direct control button for the camera drive, located on the top of the camera in the bottom left position, and hold it while turning the Control dial to set your drive to single or to continuous ⧉ . You can also use this setting to activate the camera's self-timer.

7. **Select your White Balance:** Use the up arrow key ⌃ to enter the White Balance mode and then use the Control dial or the arrow keys to select a white balance setting. (Try Auto if you're just getting the hang of the camera).

8. **Set an image review time:** Using the steps above, set the camera's image review time to a length that's long enough for you to check out your last shot, but not so long that it drains battery power. (And remember, you can always check your images at any time by hitting the "play" button on the left edge of the LCD screen.

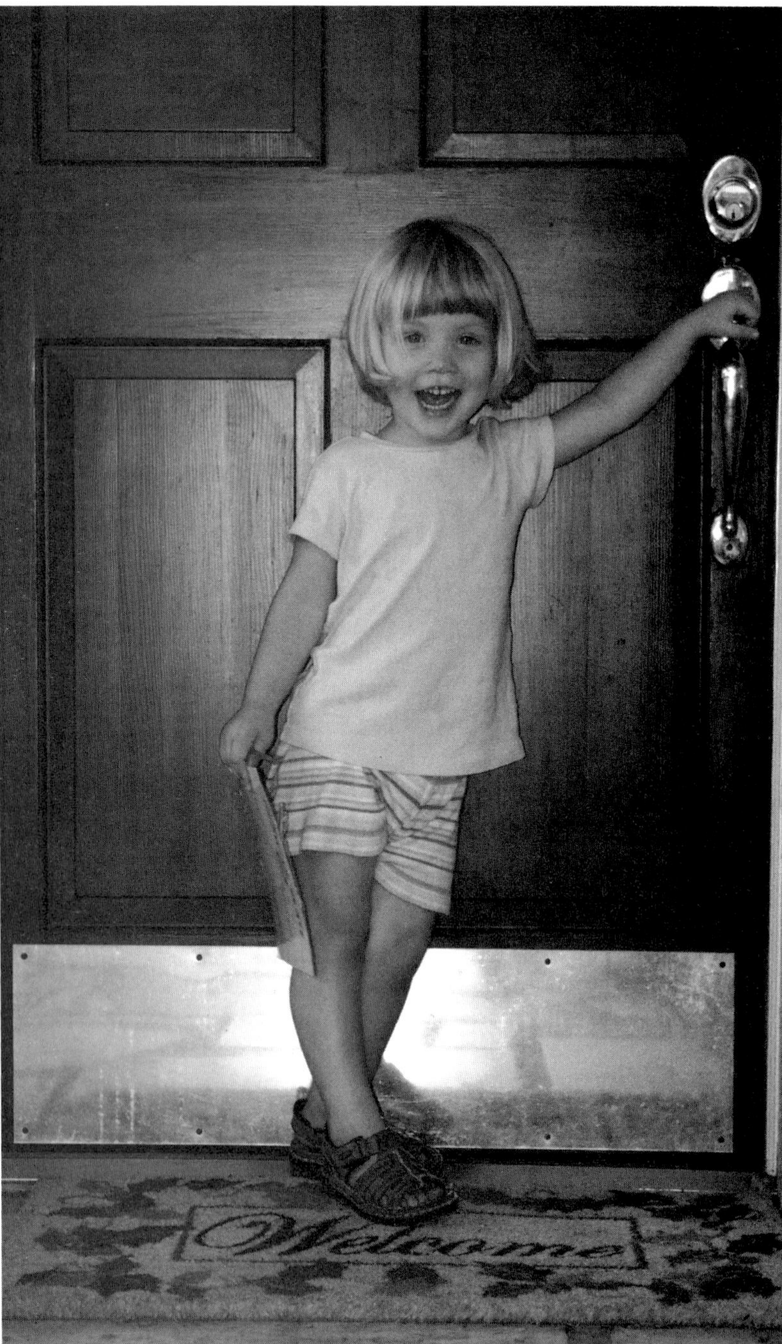
Welcome

File Formats and White Balance

As we discussed previously, the E-510 can capture images as JPEG files, as a raw file using Olympus's ORF raw format, or it can capture both of these files at the same time in a mode on the menu found as <RAW+JPEG>. This setting captures both a raw file and a JPEG file every time the shutter release is pressed.

Raw files have some advantages for the serious photographer, since they contain all the original data that comes from the sensor, and since the sensor can capture more information than the human eye can see, raw files provide unmatched post-shooting editing possibilities.

A JPEG file is designed to be small and it's a compressed file that throws away some of the photographic information based on the level of the compression. Even a high-quality JPEG file with little compression still discards any information that's not directly contained in the settings of your aperture and shutter speed. In other words, when you press the shutter release while shooting a JPEG, the extra data that the sensor captures is thrown away.

With raw files it's possible to make changes to white balance, exposure, highlight, shadow, and more without creating a file that suffers from bad looking image artifacts, because there's extra data to work with.

⇦ *The E-510 offers many image file options, which perfectly fit the needs of casual shooters, serious amateurs, or professional photographers. Photo ©M. Morgan*

A Big Bit of Difference

The primary reason that a raw file is more flexible has to do with how many "bits" the file contains. A bit is simply the smallest amount of information any digital system can store. Both JPEG and raw files store information for each the red, green, and blue channels.

The more bits something has, the more colors it can represent. The E-510 is capable of capturing 12-bits of information per channel. That means that for each color in visible light (red, green, and blue) the camera can record 4096 "shades" of color. A raw file contains that complete range of colors. A JPEG file however is only eight bit, so it can only contain 256 shades of each color.

Think of this like a box of crayons: Imagine you have the small 16 color box of crayons and you're making a picture of a sunset, it would be hard to make an accurate representation of how beautiful the scene was, right? Now instead you've got the big 256 color box. Suddenly your picture can look much more accurate.

In this case we're talking about the difference between 256 colors for each of the primary colors vs. more than 4000 of each. You can get a lot more accurate picture with those 16 bits of info because the 4096 color set can create more accurate and smaller "steps" between colors. (There might be 100 shades between very similar colors, while an eight bit file only has one.) When you go to adjust you images later and you're trying to tweak the colors, those steps make it much more likely you'll be able to subtly adjust one color without making it look like another (wrong) one.

Size Matters

There are, of course, some advantages to working with a JPEG file. Being smaller, JPEG images write more quickly to the storage media. All cameras have an internal buffer, a memory space that files sit in during the brief time between when they're captured and when they get written to a CF or xD card. This buffer can fill up quickly and until it's empty, you can't shoot any more images—pressing the shutter release will have no effect.

When shooting in raw the E-510 can hold seven frames in its internal buffer before it fills up and has to pause to write to a storage card but when shooting in the JPEG SQ mode (Standard Quality) with a fast CF card it's possible to continue shooting at the camera's three-frames-per-second speed until the card fills up.

This speed is largely in part to the new image processing engine in the E-510, the computational brains that performs the heavy lifting work turning incoming light into a string of numerical values that are written to the memory card.

The Advantage of High Speed Memory

Memory cards come with a speed rating, a numerical value that indicates how quickly they write. Most of them use a rating like "133x" and the higher the number, the faster the memory card functions. (Some companies, notably SanDisk do not use this ratings system, so it's necessary to look on their sites or literature to determine the speed of the cards.)

A fast memory card allows the E-510 to write out images at the fastest possible rate, preventing a full buffer and allowing you to shoot more continually. There's nothing worse than getting ready to take the next shot and finding that your buffer is full.

Combined with smart selection of your chosen file format you can really push this envelope. We took the E-510 and put in a top-of-the-line Lexar 300x CF card and then set the camera to <RAW> shooting mode, capturing only a raw file with no accompanying JPEG. Instead of the claimed seven frames we were able to capture ten before the buffer started to fill and rather than stopping the camera simply dropped to a continuous rate of around a frame-per-second and just kept going.

Even at the SHQ mode (the highest JPEG mode) we were able to get nearly thirty shots from the camera before the buffer showed signs of filling, at which point the speed throttled back slightly. A 60x or 80x would have filled up more quickly and would have taken longer to get back up to speed.

Now, if you don't plan to shoot images at three-frames-per-second, then it's not so important to spend more money for a higher speed card. Landscape, macro and formal-portrait shooters rarely fire off a blast of images so the added expense of a faster card isn't practical at that point. But it's good to keep in mind if you're shooting sports, weddings, or other fast-moving events.

Setting Your File Format

The camera's shooting file format can be set either with the Menu or with the camera's on-screen shooting guide.

The first method is to select the file format via the menu, though this takes a few more steps than the on-screen method (below). Press the Menu button to call up the E-510's configuration menus and the selection will be on the first shooting menu . Press the right arrow button to move to the second column and press the down arrow button to scroll down to the icon that looks like a diamond dissolving into dots. This is the new universal symbol for file format because it represents a high-quality image (the left "solid" part of the diamond) dissolving into a lower-quality, pixilated version of the diamond on the right. Get it?

Press the right arrow to move to the third column and use the up and down arrow buttons to select your desired resolution. Your options are <RAW>, <SHQ>, <HQ>, and <SQ>. Raw is, of course, the ORF Olympus raw file, SHQ is a "super high quality" JPEG, HQ is a "high quality" JPEG, while SQ is a "standard quality" JPEG. You additionally have options for a raw file plus any of the JPEG formats, so <RAW+SHQ>, <RAW+HQ>, and <RAW+SQ>.

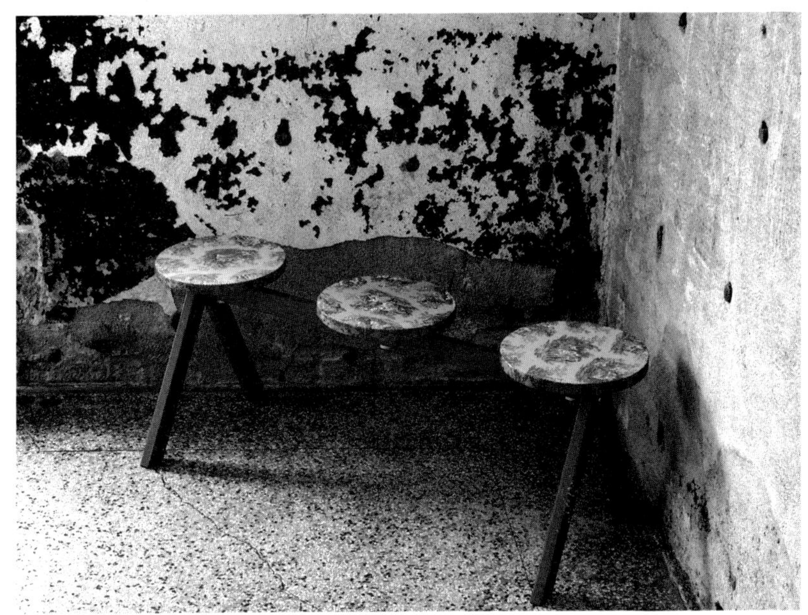

The Evolt E-510 offers many different file format settings. To get the most from your camera, choose raw or high-quality JPEG. Photo ©Kevin Kopp

Alternately, while the camera is on, if the Basic or Detailed shooting info screens are not visible, press the OK button (OK) to call up the display. On the bottom row of the menu (either the Basic or Detailed) directly next to the remaining shot counter is an option for file resolution. This will be set to whatever the current file mode is (for example, if you're shooting in HQ, that box will show <HQ>,) so simply use the arrow keys to highlight that square and then use the Control dial to change the setting. You can also press the OK button while this field is highlighted and bring up the file resolution menu, but it's usually quicker to use the Control dial.

Image Size, Quality, and Capacity

Each of the various file formats possible with the E-510 creates a file of different size file. The SQ "standard quality" format creates the smallest file while the raw file is the largest. As the levels of quality increase, so too does the size of the file. That's because information is thrown away to create the smaller sized files, so the larger the file is, the more information it contains. Shoot in a raw+JPEG mode and you'll get both a large raw file and a JPEG file. Ideally every photograph would be stored at the highest quality possible, but there's a tradeoff in size and storage. Even though memory card prices drop regularly, they're still an expense and so many photographers have to weight the benefits of shooting in various modes.

It's also possible to change settings for the JPEG SQ and HQ modes. (It's not possible to change the SHQ setting as that's already a format with the very least amount of compression possible and is a fixed compression rate.) Press the Menu button and scroll down to the first setup menu 1 and use the right arrow to move to the second column. Select <HQ> and then use the right arrow to move to the third column and choose between the <1/4>, <1/8>, and <1/12> settings.

The higher the number on the bottom, the greater the compression, and therefore the smaller your image will be. However, remember that the smaller your image the more information is throw away, decreasing the quality of your image.

By selecting the <SQ> mode in the Menu you can change both the size and the compression level of your JPEGs shot in the standard quality mode. This is particularly handy for <RAW+SQ> where you'll only be using the JPEG file as a small thumbnail to send to a client. This can be set from a maximum of full size <3200x2400> to the smallest <640x480> and then the compression can be set independently.

Size also affects image quality, so if you make a SQ image with a low compression rate and small size, you'll end up with two levels of image quality degradation, though a very small file.

One thing to keep in mind though is that storage prices regularly drop (or more accurately, larger capacity drives become available at the same price as the drives they are replacing, which forces the pricing down on all other drives) and so photographers who select a low-size (and therefore low quality) JPEG file to conserve space on their computers end up years down the road with plenty of hard drive space and a wish for higher-resolution images.

If you shoot a raw and JPEG image simultaneously, the raw file will open by default using whatever the settings were for your JPEG image, but the raw file can be adjusted to change the white balance, exposure, color saturation, and more, without losing any information in the file. The JPEG meanwhile isn't as flexible. Shoot a JPEG as a sepia image, for example, and it's always going to be a sepia image.

Many photographers take advantage of this dual raw and JPEG shooting mode to provide the maximum creative freedom but still allow for fast use of the images. Many will send the smaller JPEG files off to clients for first approval (the small size makes them easy to send via email or post to the web) and then use the raw files to create the high-resolution version, once the client has approved the JPEG.

Non-pros can take advantage of these features too, using the JPEG files for things like direct printing to compatible 4x6 inch (10x15 cm) printers while using the raw file to output a high-resolution print to hang on the wall.

Processing Raw Files

There are a variety of programs available that let you extend creative control over your raw files. A free piece of software, Olympus Master 2 will allow you to organize and work with your files, including your raw files, as will other free packages such as Apple's iPhoto, Google's Picassa, and others.

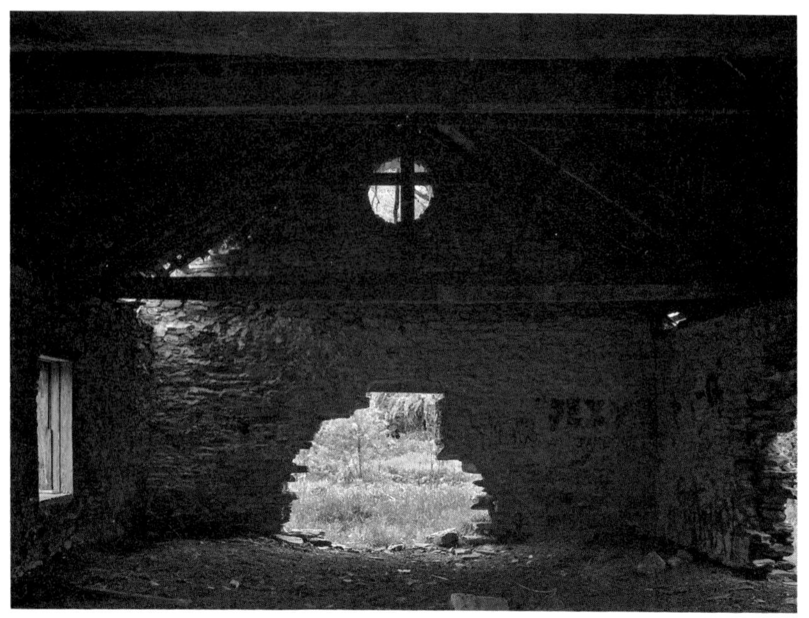

Shooting raw gives you more flexibility in image processing. It allows greater latitude in adjusting exposure, white balance, and contrast. Photo ©Kevin Kopp

Photographers looking for more professional tools often turn to programs like Apple's Aperture, Adobe's Lightroom, and Adobe Photoshop in order to get the most out of their images, especially their raw images.

Regardless of the software you use, it's possible to take the raw files from the E-510 and create stunning output, be it for web or print, thanks to the high-quality processing engine in the camera and the 4/3 imaging sensor.

All of the raw processing packages allow you to enhance and correct your images with previously unparalled control. It's possible to adjust the exposure of your images, correct white balance issues (see the White Balance section below, recover data from highlights and shadows, crop, adjust colors, fix redeye and more.

They'll also allow you to make many of these corrections to JPEG images as well, but again changes made to JPEG images degrade the overall quality of the file, while raw adjustments to not. Best of all, the new breed of raw software (namely Aperture and Lightroom) allow you to make non-destructive changes to your raw images, meaning that you can go back at any time and undo or tweak your edits, without affecting the image, and without having to create multiple save-as versions.

It's really a great time in the world of raw photography, and the Olympus ORF file contains a huge amount of photographic power.

White Balance

In the world of digital photography, there are two key camera settings to optimize one's image quality. The first is the file format, and we've already tackled that. The second is white balance, and it's especially crucial if you're shooting in a JPEG-only workflow.

First, it's crucial to understand what white balance is, and for that we need a quick trip to the human eye. As we mentioned earlier in the book, humans are designed to be able to see under a variety of lighting conditions. As the light in our world changes, colors shift and look differently. This is most visible at sunset as the world takes on a warm glow that changes and evolves as the sun goes down. Since the "color" of the light from the sun is continually changing at sunset, our eyes perceive the color cast.

A world in which a person got eaten by a tiger because the tiger looked different between dusk and afternoon would be a world devoid of people, so the brain learned to adapt to the changes.

Cameras don't adapt, per-se, but they can be adjusted to be sensitive to different wavelengths of light. In fact, it's important to tell your camera what color "white" is, because that will be the starting point for every other color the camera "sees." If the white balance isn't set correctly all the colors in your image will be incorrect. It's a relatively trivial matter to change this in a raw file, but it can be a painful or impossible experience with a JPEG image.

White balance is measured in what's called "color temperature" with a scale called Kelvin. (Any scientists familiar with absolute zero have already met Kelvin). It's a really geeky way to describe if a light source is bluish or reddish. Light sources with a lower Kelvin temperature appear more red, higher temperature lights appear bluer. (Go figure.) Normal daylight sun is about 5200K, for comparison sake.

The E-510 features a very powerful Auto white balance setting, which is great for the majority of shooting situations but there are some things to remember. When accurate color is critical the auto white balance can result in slightly different colors from frame to frame. Many photographers also prefer the preset and custom white balance settings as they provide more consistent, and often more accurate color. (That's because the auto setting picks the lightest part of the image and treats it as white, even if it's not.)

The different white balance settings are easy to use and worth exploring, as they give great and consistent results. Access the white balance controls by pressing the up arrow any time the camera is on with a blank LCD screen. Alternately you can press the OK button to bring up the shooting information screen and use the arrow keys to highlight the white balance settings, which is the second from the left on the first row of choices.

The E-510 offers preset white balances for direct sun **5300K**, shade **7500K**, cloudy skies **6000K**, tungsten lighting **3000K**, and then three fluorescent settings **1 4000K** **2 4500K** **3 6600K** for standard fluorescent, neutral white balanced fluorescent and then finally daylight balanced fluorescent.

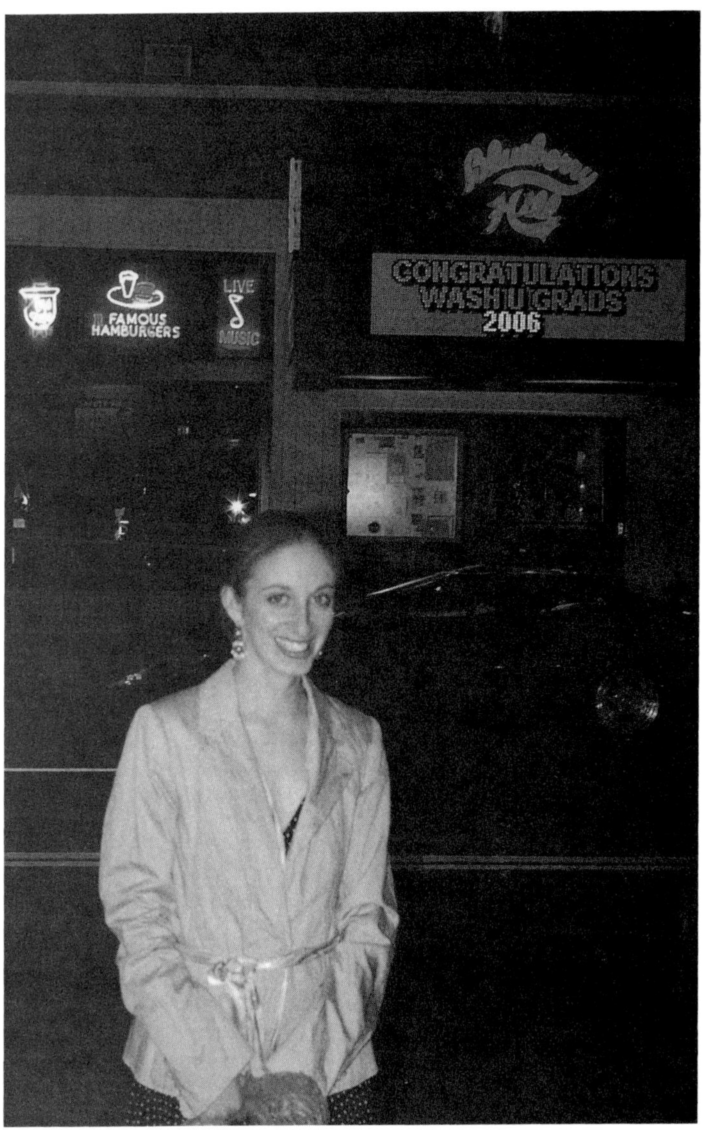

When setting white balance consider the overall creative effect. In this case, the cloudy skies white balance preset was chosen to both warm the flash-lit subject and the neon lights behind. Photo ©M. Morgan

White Balance Presets

AUTO **Auto:** This mode sets the color based on a complex series of conditions that basically boil down to setting the lightest part of the image to being "white." Color temperature in this range will usually be between 3000-7000K. Lacking a real white point to make a color judgment, auto white balance modes might display colors differently from image to image.

It's a good mode if you're in a hurry, but it's often better to pick one of the color modes below, especially if you're shooting in raw where you can go back and edit your white balance after the shot.

5300K **Daylight:** Daylight, as mentioned above, is about 5200K and it represents typical light in non-sunrise or sunset parts of the day. (Usually about 10am until 4pm.)

7500K **Shade:** This setting, around 7000K is best for shooting objects that are out of direct sunlight, eliminating the blue cast they might have with the daylight setting. Many photographers use this setting to warm up a scene that's shot under blue skies.

6000K **Cloudy:** At about 6000K the cloudy setting is also great for dusk and sunset. It warms up cloudy days (which tend to be a bit blue) but by a smaller amount than the shade setting does. Many photographers leave their camera in the cloudy setting as they like the warm cast it provides. It's also a great setting to bring out the warm colors of a sunrise or sunset.

3000K **Tungsten:** This setting at about 3200K gives a daylight-look to images shot under tungsten lighting. It removes the yellowish cast that's associated with shooting under normal household bulbs. It's also possible to use this to add a bluish cast to daylight images, such as snow scenes, for a creative effect.

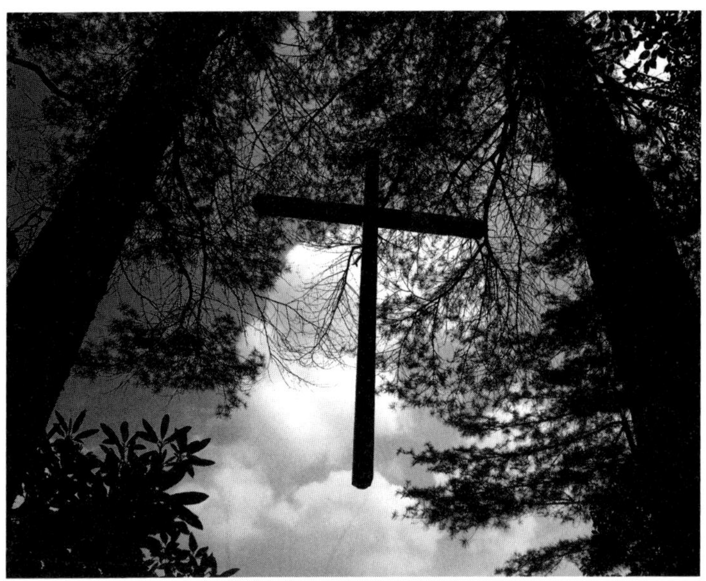

The Daylight white balance preset is ideal for outdoor shots in the middle hours of the day. Photo ©Kevin Kopp

1 4000K 2 4500K 3 6600K **Fluorescent light:** The E-510 has three different fluorescent settings for the three common types of fluorescent bulbs found today. Ranging between 4000K and 6600K they have specific applications. Generally the first setting, the one for the standard fluorescent bulb is the most helpful, as that type of bulb provides the least flattering (and hardest to correct) green tint.

TIP: Most cameras have a white balance setting for flash, but the E-510 is lacking that setting. Luckily that setting is right about 6000K, so it's possible to use the Cloudy setting to balance out the effects of a flash system or the built-in flash.

Custom: The custom settings (either the one-touch, covered below or the direct-entry method) allow the photographer to create the perfect white balance for the lighting at hand. The direct entry mode is particularly handy when shooting under a controlled lighting environment (like halogen or sodium vapor lights) where the color temperature is known.

The one-touch mode provides a simple solution for creating the perfect white balance, but it requires assigning the Function button **Fn** found on the back of the camera just below the Control dial, to be assigned to the one-touch WB mode. Here's how to do that:

- First, press the Menu button and bring up the first setup menu by scrolling down with the arrow keys. Press the right arrow to move to the second column and scroll down to the <FN FUNCTION> screen Fn . Press the right arrow key, which puts you in the column to assign a special feature to the function button. Use the up or down arrows to scroll until you see <One touch WB> displayed and then press the OK button.

- Depress the shutter release half way to enter shooting mode.

- Next, access the white balance mode by pressing up on the arrow pad and selecting the one-touch white balance setting .

- Hold down the Fn key on the back of the camera and the LCD display will prompt you to point the camera at a white sheet of paper. Make sure there are no shadows on the paper, as that can throw off the white balance mode.

- Press the shutter release and take your picture. The camera displays your image for review (remember, no shadows) and pressing OK sets that as the new white balance point.

TIP: Remember, if you move from one light source to another (like moving from outside to inside) you'll need to create a new custom white balance, or use one of the presets.

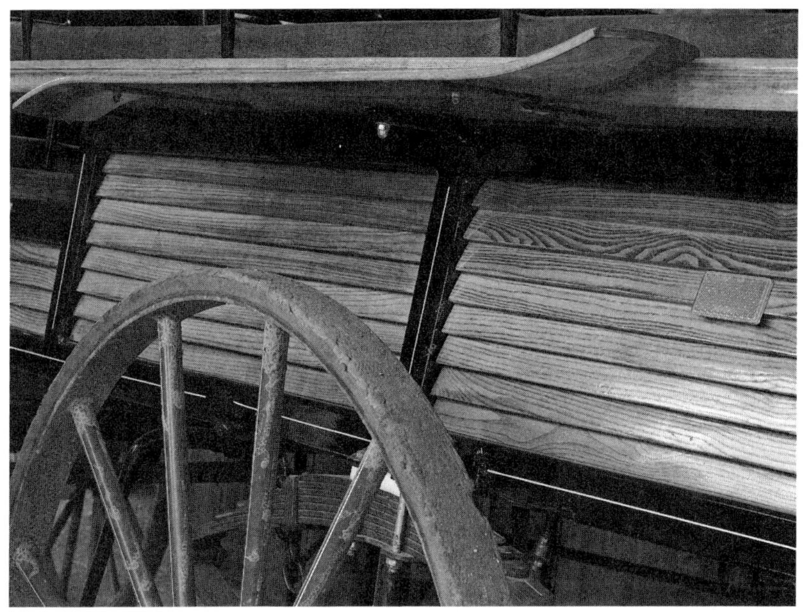

The one-touch white balance mode facilitates taking a custom reading off a white piece of paper. This is the traditional way that white balance was set on early video cameras, and it is very useful when color fidelity is critical. Photo ©Kevin Kopp

To change the custom white balance through the direct-entry method, press the Menu button to go to the first shooting menu. Press the right arrow to enter the first shooting menu and use the down arrow to highlight the <WB> selection. Press the right arrow again to enter the white balance settings, and scroll using the down arrow until the custom white balance <CWB> selection is highlighted. Press the right arrow to enter the custom white balance settings, and use the up and down arrows to choose a specific Kelvin temperature (the setting changes in increments of 50 K). Press OK to make your selection.

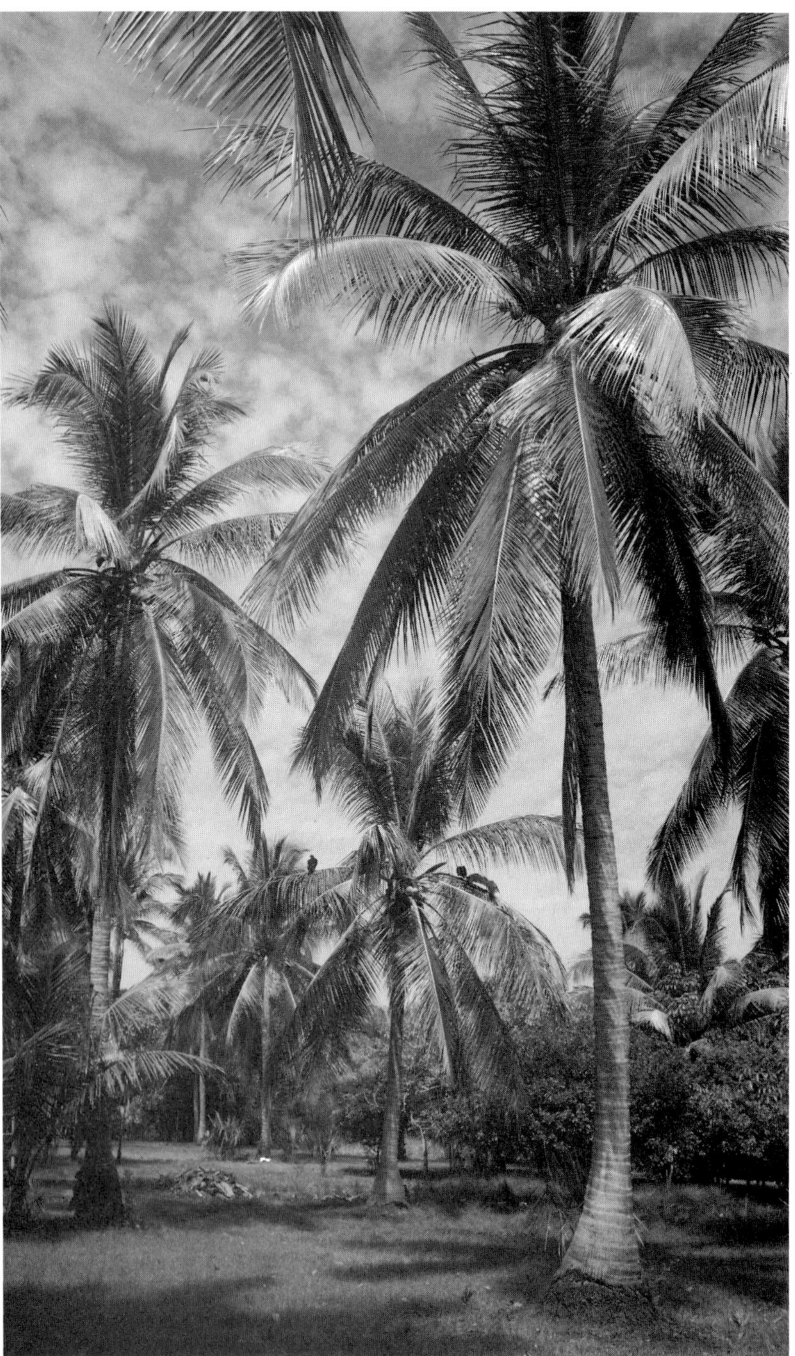

Camera and LCD Menus

Just about every digital camera on the market uses some sort of menu system to configure camera settings. While film cameras were easy to set (put in a roll of film, set the ISO if it wasn't read automatically, and shoot) digital cameras have an amazing amount of options and features available. This has been a tremendous boon to the photographer, all the bells-and-whistles found in today's digital camera were unheard of just a few years ago.

Of course, every rose has its thorns and the added sophistication of today's digital cameras can often cause confusion even for those familiar with the digital landscape. Add to this the fact that the E-510 achieves its compact shape in part by eliminating the top LCD screen found on many cameras, and instead provides a dual set of menu options, and the result can be a confusing experience.

Luckily the E-510 is relatively easy to master, once you know where to look. Even better, most camera functions can be accessed either via the Main menu, the Control menu, or the Direct menu. (For clarity, we're calling the options viewed when the Menu button is pressed the "Main menu" and the screens accessed via the OK button or the info button the "Control menu," and any combination of hitting the arrow keys the "Direct menu."

The E-510's extensive menu system expands the versatility of the camera and its controls. It allows photographers to tailor the camera to every shooting requirement.

The Direct menu is the place most photographers will start (and the easiest menu to activate) so we'll begin with those features.

Direct Menu

By pressing the four arrow buttons Fn it's possible to directly access many of the most common shooting features. This is the easiest way to jump directly to the necessary settings without running into a lot of clutter. Mastering the Direct menu will make most shooting tasks much easier.

Each direct selection works the same way—press one of the arrow buttons to enter a selection mode, then either use the control dial or use the left and right arrow keys to move through the selections. Press the OK button or half-press the shutter release to make your selection.

Up Arrow **White Balance** **WB** : Auto AUTO, Sunny 5300K, shade 7500K, cloudy 6000K, tungsten 3000K, fluorescent 1 4000K, fluorescent 2 4500K, fluorescent 3 6600K, one-touch custom , custom CWB.

Right Arrow **Autofocus** **AF** : Single AF <S-AF> (locks focus and takes picture), continuous <C-AF> (tracks subject and takes shot whenever shutter is press, without locking focus first), manual focus <MF> (uses the focus ring on the lens to focus), single AF plus manual <S-AF + M> (either single focus or manual ring), continuous focus plus manual <C-AF+M> (either continuous focus or manual ring).

Down Arrow **ISO** **ISO** : Auto, 100, 200, 400, 800, 1600

Left Arrow **Metering** : Digital ESP ESP (uses the whole viewfinder and intelligently makes metering choices), center weighted , spot , spot high (use if spot metering on a very bright scene) HI, spot shadow SH (use if spot metering on a shadowy scene).

While they're not part of the arrow-based Direct menu, another set of very handy buttons for direct settings are the autofocus button [···] found directly under the Control dial and the image stabilization button IS found to the right of the LCD screen.

Pressing the autofocus button brings up the AF area selector, which sets the camera to automatically pick the best of the three focus areas, or to use the right, middle, or left area.

Likewise, hitting the IS button brings up the image stabilization options (see page 43) for selection of image stabilization modes.

Control Menu

The Control menu is activated by pressing the OK button on the rear of the camera (in the center of the arrow buttons) or by pressing the Info button while the E-510 is on with an idle LCD screen. (In other words not reviewing an image or being used for the Direct menu.)

Pressing the OK button will bring up the Control menu, as will the Info button, but pressing the Info button a second time will switch between the basic and the detailed menus.

Both the basic and the detailed Control menus feature a slightly confusing interface. Here's how it works: The Control menus display all the camera settings. If you press the Info button you will only be able to view the current set of settings. Press the Info button a second time to toggle between the basic and detailed. However, to change any of the settings it's necessary to first press the OK button, which will highlight one of the available info fields. (The field last modified will be the starting place each time you press the OK button.)

If instead of pressing the Info button you press the OK button the Control menu will be immediately available for access to changing the settings, but pressing the Info button won't toggle between the two menu types, it'll just dismiss the Control menu.

Once the basic or detailed menu is up, use the left and right arrow buttons to scroll between the choices on a row and use the up and down arrow buttons to move between the rows of choices.

When you've landed on the parameter you'd like to change, use the control dial to change the options. For example, if you want to change the ISO, (which is the first box of the first row) hit the OK button and then make sure the ISO box is highlighted. Turn the Control dial until the correct ISO selection appears.

Basic Menu

Once the Basic menu is called up via the Info or the OK button (as described above) it's possible to move to any of the menu choices with the arrow buttons (left and right move between columns, up and down move within a column) and then turn the control dial to get the setting you want.

Basic Mode

Column One

ISO ISO : AUTO, 100, 200, 400, 800, 1600

Metering: Digital ESP ESP (uses the whole viewfinder and intelligently makes metering decisions), center weighted , spot , spot high HI (use if spot metering a very bright scene), spot shadow SH (use if spot metering a shadowy scene).

Card: CF, XD xD

Column Two

WB WB : Auto AUTO , sunny 5300K, shade 7500K, cloudy 6000K, tungsten 3000K, fluorescent 1 1 4000K, fluorescent 2 2 4500K, fluorescent 3 3 6600K, one-touch custom , custom CWB .

Autofocus Area: Auto , Left, Center, Right.

Resolution/Quality: RAW+SHQ, RAW+HQ, RAW+SQ, RAW, SHQ, HQ, SQ.

Basic Mode

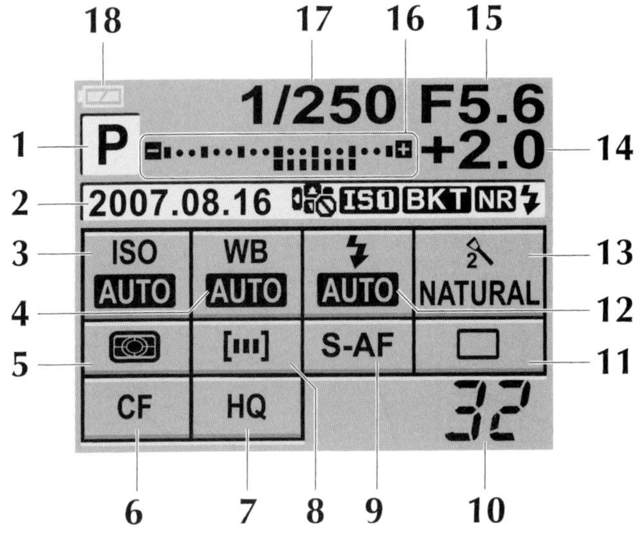

1. *Exposure mode*
2. *Date/Arrow pad lock/Image stabilizer/Auto bracketing/ Noise reduction/Flash stand-by/Internal temper- ture warning*
3. *ISO*
4. *White balance*
5. *Metering mode*
6. *Card*
7. *Record mode*
8. *AF frame*
9. *AF mode*
10. *Number of storable still pictures*
11. *Sequential shooting/ Self-timer/Remote control*
12. *Flash mode*
13. *Picture mode*
14. *Exposure compensation value*
15. *Aperture value*
16. *Exposure compensation indicator/Exposure level indicator/Flash intensity level indicator*
17. *Shutter speed*
18. *Battery check*

Column Three

Flash Mode: Auto flash **AUTO**, red-eye , fill flash , no flash , slow sync redeye reduction **SLOW**, slow first curtain sync **SLOW** (captures both background and foreground), slow second curtain **SLOW2**, manual flash full **FULL**, 1/4 full manual **1/4**, 1/16 full manual **1/16**, 1/64 full manual **1/64**.

Autofocus Mode: Autofocus **AF** : Single AF <S-AF> (locks focus and takes picture), continuous <C-AF> (tracks subject and takes shot whenever shutter is press, without locking focus first), manual focus <MF> (uses the focus ring on the lens to focus), single AF plus manual <S-AF + M> (either single focus or manual ring), continuous focus plus manual <C-AF+M> (either continuous focus or manual ring).

Column Four

Picture Mode: Vivid,natural , muted , monotone

Shooting Mode: Single shot, Drive, 12 second timer, two second timer, remote control.

Advanced Mode

The advanced much mode is more complex as it is broken down into columns as well, but several of the boxes in the columns have sub-boxes of unrelated choices.

The controls of the columns are:

Column One

ISO **ISO** : AUTO, 100, 200, 400, 800, 1600

Flash Mode: Auto flash **AUTO**, redeye , fill flash , no flash , slow sync redeye reduction **SLOW**, slow first curtain sync **SLOW** (captures both background and foreground), slow second curtain **SLOW2**, manual flash full **FULL** , 1/4 full manual **1/4** , 1/16 full manual **1/16** , 1/64 full manual **1/64** .

Exposure Compensation (EV) : Although this feature is available via a direct access button just behind the shutter release, this powerful tool is also available via the detailed menu. Exposure compensation allows you to dial in a correction to the built-in metering system, which is often fooled by overly dark or overly bright subjects. Dialing in an exposure compensation value of up to two stops in either direction can help compensate for a scene that would otherwise be over or underexposed.

Card: CF,XD **xD**

Advanced Mode

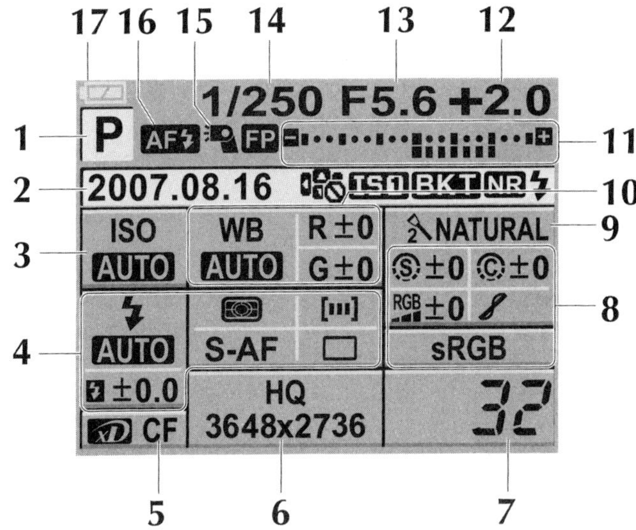

1. *Exposure mode*
2. *Date/Arrow pad lock/Image stabilizer/Auto bracketing/ Noise reduction/Flash stand-by/Internal temper-ture warning*
3. *ISO*
4. *Flash mode/Flash intensity control/Metering mode/AF mode/AF frame/Sequential shooting/Self-timer/Remote control*
5. *Card*
6. *Record mode/Pixel count*
7. *Number of storable still pictures*
8. *Color space/Sharpness/ Contrast/Saturation/ Gradation*
9. *Picture mode*
10. *White balance/White balance compensation*
11. *Exposure compensation indicator/Exposure level indicator/Flash intensity level indicator*
12. *Exposure compensation value*
13. *Aperture value*
14. *Shutter speed*
15. *Super FP flash*
16. *AF illuminator*
17. *Battery check*

Column Two

WB **WB** : Auto AUTO , Sunny 5300K, shade 7500K, cloudy 6000K, tungsten 3000K, fluorescent 1 4000K, fluorescent 2 4500K, fluorescent 3 6600K, one-touch custom , custom CWB .

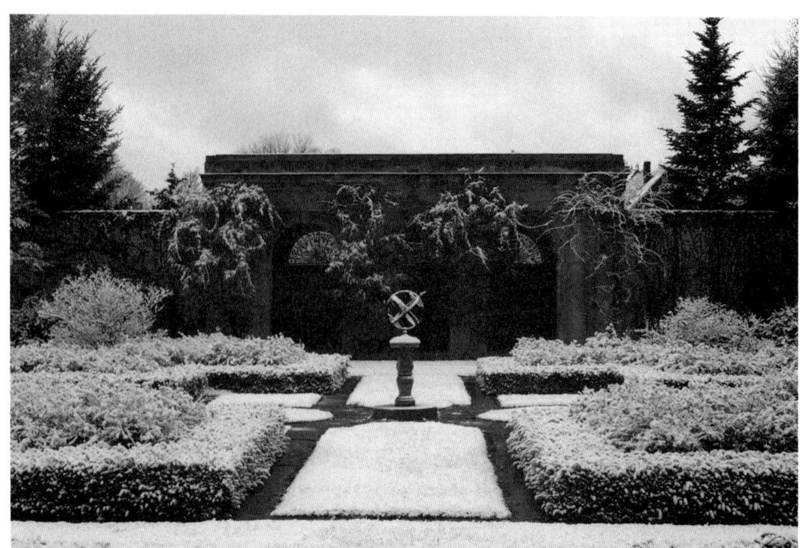

Choose Digital ESP metering for an accurate appraisal of exposure for the majority of photos you will shoot. It is highly sophisticated and will provide the highest percentage of success. Photo © M. Morgan

Metering: Digital ESP ESP (uses the whole viewfinder and intelligently makes metering decisions), center weighted , spot , spot high HI (use if spot metering a very bright scene), spot shadow SH (use if spot metering a shadowy scene).
Autofocus Mode: Autofocus **AF** : Single AF <S-AF> (locks focus and takes picture), continuous <C-AF> (tracks subject and takes shot whenever shutter is press, without locking focus first), manual focus <MF> (uses the focus ring on the lens to focus), single AF plus manual <S-AF + M> (either single focus or manual ring), continuous focus plus manual <C-AF+M> (either continuous focus or manual ring).
Resolution/Quality: RAW+SHQ, RAW+HQ, RAW+SQ, RAW, SHQ, HQ, SQ

Column Three
Red: This menu item is actually combined with the green item, below. Selecting this setting allows for adjustment of

either the red or green balance of an image, using the right and left arrows to jump between the sliders, and the up and down arrows to adjust the sliders.
Green: See above.
Autofocus Area: Auto [···], Left, Center, Right.

Column Four
Picture Mode (This spans the top of column Five) :
Vivid,natural , muted, monotone
Sharpness : Adjusting this slider changes the sharpness of the images captures from low to high by two stops in each direction.
Saturation RGB : Adjusting this slider changes the saturation of the images captures from low to high by two stops in each direction.
Color Space: A color space is like a container for all the colors that can be represented by a certain device. The sRGB space is used by most computer monitors, while the Adobe RGB space has more colors and is good if your images are going to be printed.

Column Six
Contrast : Adjusting this slider changes the saturation of the images captures from low to high by two stops in each direction.
Gradation : Adjusts the balance of tone gradients in an image. Choices are high key L , low key H, and normal . High key is useful for images with images with a lot of highlight, low key for images with a lot of shadow and normal for standard images.

Main menu

The Main menu system in the E-510 is split into five sections—two shooting menus, a playback menu and two setup menus, grouped according to the features to which they provide access. Pressing the Menu button at any time (when the camera is on) brings up the Main menu system. These controls provide direct access to many of the camera functions, most of which are duplicated by either the Direct menu or the Control menu.

Using the up and down arrow keys it's possible to scroll through the different menu sections. Once on a section you'd like to modify, press the right arrow buttons to move to the next column in the menu system. Again, using the up and down arrow keys scroll up or down until the desired feature is highlighted. Use the right arrow to move to the third column and then use the up and down arrows to scroll between the options. Press the OK button to confirm your choice or hit Menu to cancel your choice.

Shooting Menu One

CARD SETUP: Erases or formats the card(s).
Options: <ALL ERASE>, <FORMAT>

CUSTOM RESET SETTING: Resets the camera to the factory settings or to presets.
Options: <RESET>, <RESET TO PRESET 1>, <RESET TO PRESET 2>.

PICTURE MODE: Sets the saturation.
Options: <VIVID> ,<NATURAL> , <MUTED> , <MONOTONE>

GRADATION: Sets the tonal balance.
Optons: <HIGH KEY>, <LOW KEY>, <NORMAL>.

RESOLUTION : Sets camera resolution.
Options: <RAW+SHQ>, <RAW+HQ>, <RAW+SQ>, <RAW>, <SHQ>, <HQ>, <SQ>

WHITE BALANCE: Allows for precise adjustment of white balance. Each option allows for adjustment of the red and green contributions in the white balance setting.
Options: <AUTO> AUTO ,<5300K> 5300K,<7500K> 7500K,<6000K> 6000K,<3000K> 3000K,<4000K> 4000K,<4500K> 4500K,<6500K> 6600K, one touch custom , <CWB> CWB .

ISO ISO : Adjusts the sensitivity of the sensor.
Options: AUTO, 100, 200, 400, 800, 1600

NOISE FILTER: Adjusts the amount of noise in standard shooting modes.
Options: <OFF>,<LOW>,<STANDARD>,<HIGH>

NOISE REDUCTION: Reduces noise in long-exposure shots.
Options: <OFF>,<ON>

Shooting Menu Two

METERING: Sets the metering system mode.
Options: Digital ESP ESP, center weighted , spot , spot high (use if spot metering on a very bright scene) HI , spot shadow SH (use if spot metering on a shadowy scene).

Flash compensation : Sets the flash to output with more or less power than determined by the flash metering system.
Options: Adjustments +2/-2 stops in 6 stop increments each direction.

<AF MODE>: Changes the auto focus shooting mode.
Options: Single AF <S-AF> continuous <C-AF, manual focus <MF>, single AF plus manual <S-AF + M>, continuous focus plus manual <C-AF+M> .

Autofocus area : Selects which of the three AF sensor zones are in use for focusing.
Options: Auto , , , .

<AE BKT>: Autoexposure bracket sets three frames to capture each time you press the shutter release, bracketing for exposure. Each selection can take three shots, varying the amount of exposure compensation (EV) varied with each shot.
Options: <3F 0.3EV> (1/3 stop in each direction), <3F 0.7 EV> (2/3 stop in each direction), <3F 1.0EV> (full stop in each direction).

<WB BKT>: White balance bracket sets a three shot bracket varying the white balance by values of Red and Blue or Green and Magenta.
Options: range from off to six steps with each setting.

<FL BKT>: Sets a three shot bracket of shots varying the flash output.
Options: <OFF>.<3F 0.3EV>, <3F 0.7EV>,<3F 1.0EV>

<ANTI-SHOCK>: Changes the amount of time after raising the mirror before the shutter trips, in order to reduce camera motion for long-exposure shots.
Options: Values range from off to 30 seconds, in one second increments.

Play Menu

Image review : Sets the number of images displayed in the LCD during playback.
Options: **1** , **4** , **9** , **16** , **25**
.

Auto rotate **:** Turns on or off auto-image rotation.

<EDIT>: Puts the camera in the built-in image editing mode.
Options: For JPEG images the available <EDIT> choices are <BLACK & WHITE>, <SEPIA>, <REDEYE FIX>, <SATURATION>, resize . Selecting any of the settings will convert the current JPEG image. For raw images the camera will apply any current camera settings; set the camera modes before editing a raw file.

Print order : Allows a series of images to be set to print to a PictBridge compatible printer for direct output.
Options: Print order, print all.

<COPY ALL>: Copies the current image.

Setup Menu One

<ISO LIMIT>: Sets the highest ISO setting the camera will select while in the Auto ISO mode.
Options: <100>,<200>,<400>

<EV STEP>: Changes the interval between aperture settings when turning the Control dial in aperture priority mode.
Options: <1/3EV>,<1/2EV>,<1EV>

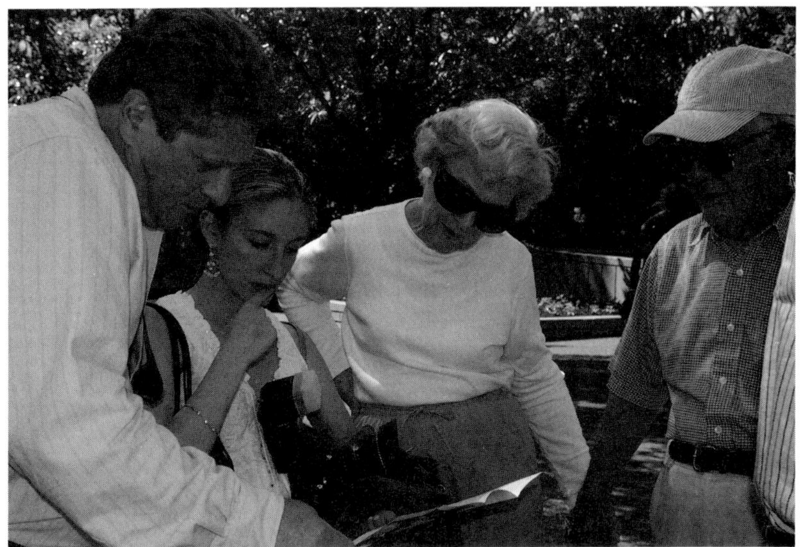

Auto ISO with a set limit of ISO 400 is a great choice for snapshot photography on very bright sunny days. The camera will automatically adjust the ISO, as needed, when subjects move from bright sun to deep shade. Photo © M. Morgan

<ALL > WB± [***NOTE:*** this menu setting, and several that follow, is a combo of the word (in this case "all") and then icon WB± : Performs a global adjustment to the white balance red and green settings.
Options: <ALL SET>(Adjust R and G with the up and down arrows,left and right to move between R and G) or <ALL RESET> (removes all global white balance adjustments).

<HQ>: Sets the compression ratio for high quality JPEGs.
Options: <1/4>,<1/8>,<1/12>

<SQ>: Sets the size and compression ratio for standard quality JPEGs.
Options: <3200x2400> to <640x480> (pixel count), <1/2.7><1/4>,<1/8>,<1/12> (compression).

< >: Link the flash compensation setting to the exposure compensation (EV)
Options: <OFF>,<ON>

<AUTO POP UP>: Controls whether or not the pop up flash activates automatically in low light.
Options: <ON>,<OFF>

<DIAL>: Changes the function of the Control dial in program and manual modes.
Options: Program Mode—<Ps> (program shift), (exposure compensation. Manual Mode—<SHUTTER> (controls shutter speed),<FNo.> (controls the aperture).

<AEL/AFL>: Specifies the use of the AEL/AFL button for either autofocus or auto exposure settings.
Options: Main options are <S-AF> (single auto focus),<C-AF>(continuous auto focus),<MF>(manual focus). Each of these options has a sub-option with between 1-4 different behaviors for the button. Follow the on-screen guide for information on each of the settings.

<AEL/AFL MEMO>: Sets the "memo" feature of the AEL/AFL button.
Options: <ON>(pressing the AEL/AFL button once locks the exposure in memory, pressing it a second time clears it from memory.),<OFF>(exposure only remains locked while the AEL/AFL button is pressed.)

<AELMetering>: Sets the metering system mode.
Options: Digital ESP ESP, center weighted , spot , spot high (use if spot metering on a very bright scene) HI, spot shadow SH (use if spot metering on a shadowy scene).

<QUICK ERASE>: Changes function of the erase button.
Options: <OFF> (when the erase button is pressed a confirmation screen appears before erasure), <ON> (images are erased without confirmation screen when erase button is pressed).

<RAW+JPEG ERASE>: Sets the behavior of the erase button when shooting in raw+JPEG mode.
Options: <JPEG>(only erases JPEG),<RAW>(only erases raw),<RAW+JPEG>(erases both images).

< Fn Function>: Controls the behavior of the function key.
Options: <PREVIEW>(triggers depth of field preview), <LIVE PREVIEW> (triggers depth of field on LCD display), <OFF> (turns off Fn button), < > (triggers one touch white balance), <TEST PICTURE> (captures an image without saving it to test settings), <MY MODE> (triggers custom user camera setting).

<MY MODE SETUP>: Provides two custom memory settings for all camera functions. Handy for temporarily switching the camera to another mode (especially when used with the function key setting for <MY MODE> above.
Options: <MY MODE 1>,<MY MODE 2> (each can be set to the current camera settings, or the mode can be reset).

<FOCUS RING>: Controls the direction used on the focus ring. < ↺ > (infinity is reached counter-clockwise), < ↻ > (infinity is reached turning clockwise).

<AF ILLUMINAT.>: Toggles the use of the built-in flash as a focus light.
Options: <ON>,<OFF>.

<RESET LENS>: Resets the focus point of the lens back to infinity when the power is switched off.
Options: <ON>,<OFF>.

<LIVE VIEW BOOST>: Adjusts brightness of LCD display during Live View shooting.
Options: <ON>(brightens image, will not display WB correction or EV),<OFF>(normal mode).

<PRIORITY RELEASE S>: Normally the E-510 will not trip the shutter while the AF is acquiring an image or is charging the flash. This setting changes that behavior in the S-AF mode (single auto focus).
Options: <ON> (trips shutter on press),<OFF>(normal behavior, waits to trip shutter).

<PRIORITY RELEASE C>: Normally the E-510 will not trip the shutter while the AF is acquiring an image or is charging the flash. This setting changes that behavior in the C-AF mode (continuous auto focus).
Options: <ON> (trips shutter on press),<OFF> (normal behavior, waits to trip shutter).

< >: Turns on or off the confirmation tone.
Options: <ON>,<OFF>.

<FRAME ASSIST>: Enables additional compositional guides when shooting in Live View mode.
Options:<OFF>, <GOLDEN SECTION> (shows guidelines according to the "golden rule" compositional design), <GRID>, <SCALE> (displays scale marks along the guidelines).

< LOCK>: Locks the arrow pad buttons during shooting.
Options: <OFF>,<ON>

Setup Menu Two
< >: Sets the time and date.

<[CF/xD]>: Switches between use of the CF and xD cards.
Options: Only active if both card slots are in use at the same time.

<FILE NAME>: The E-510 can either consecutively number images across multiple storage cards or reset the numbering each time a new card is inserted. This setting toggles this behavior.
Options: <AUTO>(keeps numbering across cards),<OFF>

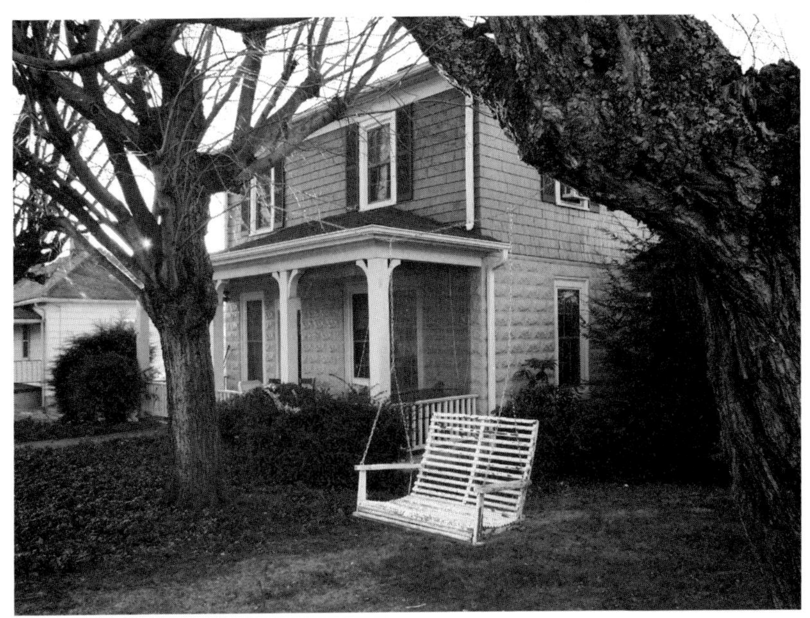

The Evolt E510 offers many choices for recording files to memory cards. It allows flexibility in how the camera names and numbers files, and will even record files to two different cards (one CF and one xD) if both are installed in the camera at the same time. Photo © M. Morgan

<EDIT FILENAME>: Allows for modifications to the camera's file naming conventions.
Options: The first letter and number can be edited for either sRGB or Adobe RGB shooting.

< >: Adjusts the brightness of the display.
Options: 15 steps between lowest and highest brightness.

< >: Sets default language of the camera menu system.
Options: <ENGLISH>.<FRANCIAS>,<ESPANOL>

<VIDEO OUT>: Switches between U.S. and European video formats.
Options: <NTSC>(U.S.), <PAL>(Europe).

<REC VIEW>: Sets the duration an image plays back on the LCD screen after capture.
Options: Durations from <1 SEC> to <20 SEC> in one second increments.

<BACKLIT LCD>: Changes the period of time after activating the menu system before the backlight dims to conserve battery power.
Options: <8 SEC>,<30 SEC>,<1 MIN>,<HOLD>.

<4 h TIMER>: Sets the camera to turn off if inactive for four hours.
Options: <OFF>,<4 h>

<BUTTON TIMER>: Sets the period of time between the last press of a button and when the camera's menu turns off.
Options: <3 SEC>,<5 SEC>,<8 SEC>,<HOLD>.

<PRIORITY SET>: Strangely named, this setting changes the default selection in the erase or format screens.
Options: <NO>(leaves the default choice to "no"), <YES> (leaves the default choice to "yes").

<USB MODE>: The built-in USB port in the E-510 can perform several functions. This setting selects the mode of operation for the USB port.
Options: <AUTO> (camera asks for mode setting each time the USB cable is connected),<STORAGE>(the mode needed for image transfer via Olympus Master software),<MTP> (this setting allows for transfer to a Vista computer, without needing Olympus Master software), <CONTROL> (enables control of the E-510 via USB and Olympus Studio software. < EASY> (allows for printing directly to a PictBridge compatible printer, without needing a PC), < CUSTOM> (prints to a PictBridge printer, using custom print settings).

<COLOR SPACE>: A color space is like a container for all the colors that can be represented by a certain device. The sRGB space is used by most computer monitors, while the Adobe RGB space has more colors and is good if your images are going to be printed.
Options: <sRGB>,<Adobe RGB>

<SHADING COMP>: This setting increases the brightness at the edge of an image to compensate for some shading that can occur with some lenses. This effect is usually found with wide angle lenses at their widest setting.
Options: <ON>,<OFF>

<PIXEL MAPPING>: Digital camera users sometimes find that over time their images end up with single pixels of red, green, or blue showing up on their images. This is due to "stuck pixels," sensor areas where the pixels are no longer responding properly. Pixel mapping checks for these stuck pixels and sets the camera to ignore them, restoring accurate images.
Options: <START> (this maps out the sensor, no further action is necessary).

<CLEANINGMODE>: This control activates the same sensor cleaning the E-510 performs on startup.
Options: <START>

<FIRMWARE>: Displays the firmware of both the camera body and currently attached lens.

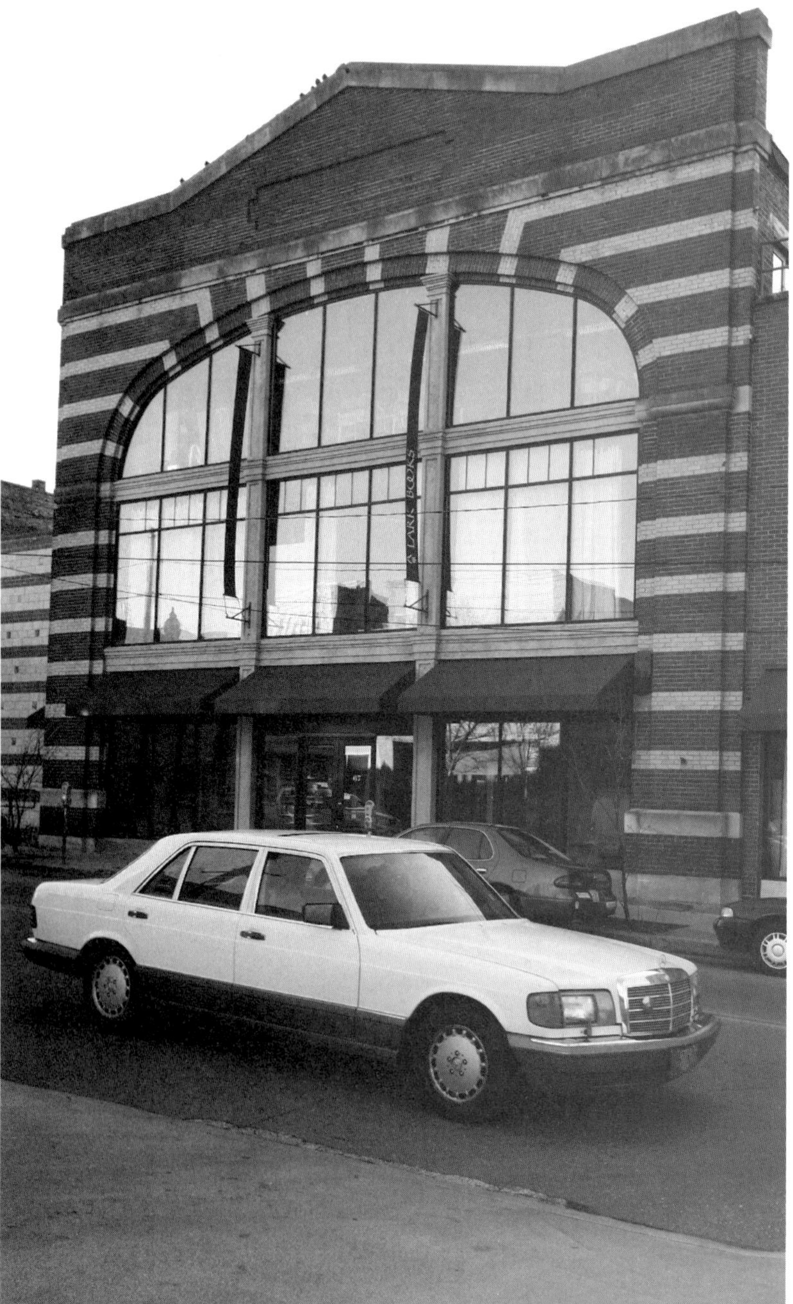
LARK BOOKS

Camera Operation Modes

The Olympus E-510 is a tremendously powerful digital camera; its small, lightweight body belies the incredibly sophisticated technology. Once you've played with the system for a while (and especially after digging through the custom camera settings in the various menus), it will become obvious that the E-510 is a contender in the serious gear category.

But the sophistication of the E-510 doesn't make it difficult to use. A variety of camera systems and operation modes combine to make the camera work as seamlessly and effortlessly on fully Manual mode as it functions on any automatic mode.

The camera's focusing and metering systems work in tandem with the various shooting modes and scene modes to help the photographer take great pictures. An understanding of the various systems will allow the photographer to get the best images possible from the E-510.

Focus System

The E-510 uses a sophisticated TTL (through-the-lens) phase-difference detection system to drive its autofocus (AF). A three-point multiple AF detection area (adjustable in the menus to work in auto mode or to select a single point) features both a single focus and continuous focus system, both of which can work with manual override for the sharpest images possible. The AF system functions between 0 and 19 EV (at ISO 100) and all three AF points are visible in the viewfinder.

⇦ *The E-510 combines sophisticated phase-difference detection focusing system with Digital ESP metering to create excellently focused and exposed images. Photo ©M. Morgan*

In real terms, this translates into an autofocus system that can operate quickly even in low light, and can lock onto a target that's moving and continue to stay focused on that target even as it moves. In S-AF mode (see pages 70-72) the camera will lock onto a subject before the shutter will trigger, while in C-AF mode the camera will continue to focus as a subject moves as long as the shutter release stays half-depressed, and will trigger the camera shutter each time the release is completely depressed. In S-AF+M and C-AF+M mode (see pages 70-72) the manual focus ring can be turned at any time for fine tuning.

In low-light shooting environments, the E-510 can use its built-in flash as a scene illuminator, lighting up a subject for focus assist. When used in tandem with one of Olympus's external flash systems (connected to the built in flash shoe) the E-510 can utilize the infrared focusing assist beam featured on the flash units to enable focus in total darkness.

By default the E-510 automatically analyzes the scene at hand and determines the most appropriate focus zone to capture the subject. Some shooting conditions can confuse or fool the autofocus system (landscapes with a prominent foreground object that isn't the subject, or a off-center portrait of a person standing nearby an object, for example) and in these cases the E-510 can be set to limit its focus to only one of the AF points. This is most easily accomplished with the direct AF point button on the rear of the camera beneath the Control dial, but it can also be changed via the camera menus. (See page 68.)

Self-Timer and Drive Modes

The E-510 offers both single-shot and continuous-shooting modes, with a three frame-per-second speed in continuous mode. A self-timer with variable durations can be used for trigger the camera and the accessory remote control can be used for remote camera triggering without the need of a shutter release cable. Both the self-timer and the remote trigger timer are great for long exposure tripod shots, since they allow the camera to be completely motion free when tripping the shutter.

The most direct access to these features is via the drive mode button found on the left side of the camera's top panel. ⧉/⏲/ǂ. Pressing this button jumps to the drive mode selection menu, with the choices of single □, continuous ⧉, 12-second timer ⏲s, two-second timer ⏲2s, remote with no delay ǂs, remote with two-second delay ǂ2s.

Exposure Settings

There is nothing that can be done to correct a photograph with a totally blown exposure. As a result, it's a good idea to master the basics of camera exposure settings: ISO, shooting mode, scene modes, exposure compensation, and bracketing.

An important rule of photography is that sensitivity, shutter speed, and aperture are all connected to each other. Many shooters understand that there's a relationship between f/stop and shutter speed, but they neglect the all-important imaging sensor ISO when evaluating a scene.

To sum up the entire art of photography in a nutshell: if you change any of these three settings on your camera you will need to change one of the other two to end up with the same amount of light striking the sensor. Changing any of the settings by a full "stop" either halves or doubles the amount of light coming into the camera, depending on which direction you make the change.

So, if you go from ISO 100 to 200 (a full stop) you double the amount of light striking the sensor. If you go from f/2.8 to f/5.6 (again, a full stop) you'll halve the light hitting the sensor. (Why do aperture settings have such odd numbers? It all has to do with the mathematics of the way light is measured, but let's just blame it instead on the Victorians. If you've ever tried to figure out a tennis match, you understand their odd numbering scheme.) Finally, if you change your shutter speed from 1/30th of a second to 1/60th of a second you'll halve the amount of light coming into the camera.

ISO

In a lot of ways, a digital camera sensor is like a microphone. A microphone doesn't care how loudly you talk into it, as long as you set the output to handle the sound volume. Talk too quietly into it though and you'll have to boost (amplify) the audio to make up for the lack of volume, and that's often where you end up with a distracting hum or static. Talk into the mic in a voice louder than the expected level and you'll get distortion and clipping.

Likewise, a digital imaging sensor doesn't care how "bright" the light is coming into it, so long as the ISO is set to match that incoming light. In order to pick up fainter detail it's necessary to turn up the signal coming from the sensor, and while that works, it can result in the visual equivalent of hum and static—noise. Give it a light that's too bright and you get the equivalent of distortion—overexposed areas.

The moral of that story is that it's necessary to set the ISO to an appropriate level, but it's also important to keep in mind that you want to try and manage your lighting conditions (as much as possible) to keep your ISO as low as you can. The higher the setting, the more the signal coming off is amplified, and so the more noise you'll get.

The E-510 offers ISO settings from 100 to 1600 and includes an Auto mode, the upper end of which is controlled via the <ISO LIMIT> menu choice. (See page 76.) The ISO settings can be accessed by pressing the down arrow any time the camera is in shooting mode and the turning the Control dial to select a ISO speed.

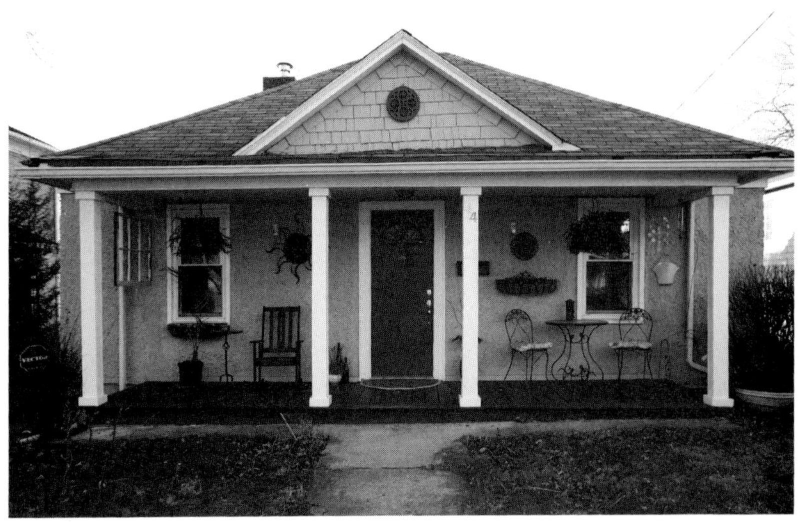

ISO ratings are international standards that are applied to film to quantitize an emulsion's sensitivity to light. While digital cameras do not have true ISOs, the numbers are still used because they are so familiar to photographers. The sensor in a digital camera has one fixed sensitivity–the various ISOs are achieved by camera electronics. Photo © M. Morgan

Metering Modes

The light meters built into modern digital cameras are fantastic, they're unbelievably better than the light meters used even ten-years ago. They work by measuring the light coming into the camera's lens and comparing that to preset instructions about how to handle those scenes. Many full-time pros rely solely on the in-camera readings provided by these metering systems.

The Evolt E-510's metering modes are most easily accessed in the Metering menu during shooting. Press the left arrow and use the Control dial to make your selection. Camera metering modes can also be set via the E-510's menu systems (see pages 75 and 78.)

Digital ESP *ESP*

The most advanced, Digital ESP metering *ESP* breaks the incoming light from the subject into 49 different zones. It evaluates the exposure for each and then compares them to determine the correct exposure. This prevents super-bright objects (the sun, streetlights) or super dark ones (deep shade, large dark objects) in a small portion of the image from distorting the overall exposure of the scene.

Still, photographers may want to utilize different metering modes to take greater control over their image creation. The E-510 offers four additional metering modes, center-weighted averaging, spot metering, spot highlight HI, and spot shadow SH.

Center Weighted

Center-weighted metering places the emphasis on the middle of the image, and evaluates the remainder of the frame to a lesser degree. This metering system was prevalent in early film SLRs, so many photographers are used to it and continue to use it. While not as sophisticated as ESP, it often provides good results when shooting a portrait with a bright background.

Spot

Spot metering only measures a very small area of the frame. This is a great mode if you're trying to capture a detail far away in a landscape without metering for the background objects. It is also useful for close-up photography or anytime you want to meter a small area in a composition. Simply place the center AF point of the viewfinder on the area you want to meter and it'll ignore the rest.

Smart Spot Metering Modes: The E-510 includes two more smart spot metering modes (not found on most cameras), the first of which (Spot highlight) is for metering something white on a bright background (a bride's dress against white seamless paper, for example.) The second Spot shadow is great for metering a dark object against a dark background (such as the groom in a tux standing in front of a black limo).

Exposure Lock

In most shooting modes, the E-510 continually re-evaluates the appropriate shutter speed and aperture as the camera refocuses, even if the shutter release button is partially depressed. This is contrary to the action of many digital SLR cameras, where the exposure is locked when the shutter button is halfway depressed, as long as the button is not released, at which point the metering system shuts off.

Since the E-510 will continually evaluate the proper shooting settings, to lock a reading, it's necessary to press the AEL/AFL button on the upper back of the camera, to the right of the viewfinder. As long as this button is depressed, the E-510 will hold the exposure settings in memory and will utilize those settings, even if lighting conditions change. This is particularly helpful if you're metering a scene where you want to expose for something that's not the primary object in the viewfinder, for example a piece of jewelry on someone's shirt. Simply point the camera at the item you'd like properly exposed, press the AEL/AFL button (and hold it) then recompose your shot, and press the shutter release button.

TIP: Keep in mind that the camera's viewfinder is actually a light-gathering instrument—any light that strikes it is evaluated by the metering system. Often this won't matter, since the photographer's eye is usually against the viewfinder, there's no additional light entering the camera's internal metering system. However, during shots where the camera is being operated remotely and the photographer is not looking through the viewfinder, this can be an issue. It's possible to get an underexposure due to light entering the camera's viewfinder. To prevent this, fit the EP-4 eyepiece cover (packaged with the E-510 camera), over the viewfinder whenever the camera is used on a tripod or other support.

Using the LCD to Judge Exposure

The LCD screen on the back of the E-510 is a very high-quality display, and it can be used as a (relatively) good evaluative tool for judging the exposure of your images. It's not perfect though. This display is less accurate and obviously smaller than even the average computer display, so it's not an ideal system for judging your images.

However, the E-510 is equipped with three evaluative functions (one of which is rarely found on other digital cameras). These are the highlight alert, the shadow alert, and the histogram. All of these features are available by pressing the Info button on the bottom left of the back of the camera while in image review mode, which in turn is accessed by pressing the play button found on the back left of the camera, at the top of the row of buttons to the left of the LCD. By pressing the Info button repeatedly, it's possible to cycle through the different image review modes (see page 39.)

The Histogram

There are two histogram modes, the first shows a histogram for each color channel in the image, and the second mode displays a single evaluative histogram of the brightness for the whole shot.

A histogram is pretty easy to read once you've gotten the hang of it. The horizontal axis represents levels of brightness across either the entire range of colors (as is seen on the white, combined histogram) or across each of the red, green and blue channels (as is seen on the individual histograms). The vertical axis represents the number of pixels in your image with that level of brightness. The idea is to get a nice distribution of values without seeing either spikes on the ends (which indicate too many pixels going to highlight or shadow, and therefore overexposed or underexposed) or seeing abrupt drop offs in the histogram, which indicates very large over or underexposure.

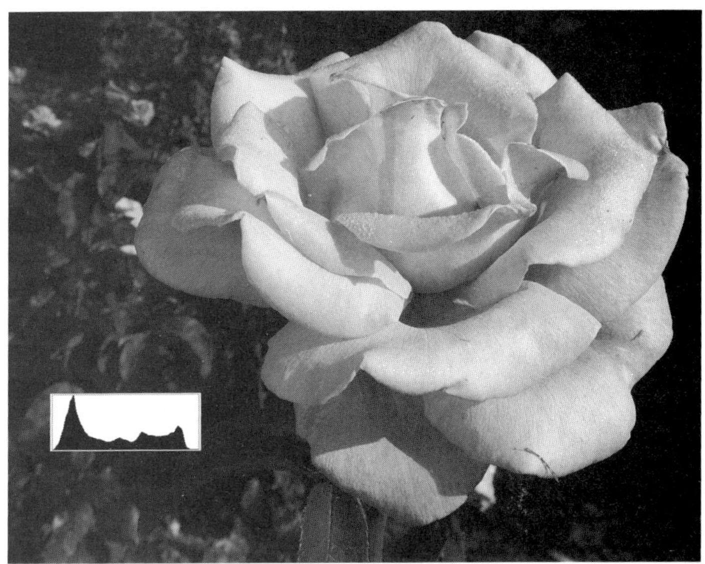

The histogram for this photo of a rose shows that there is detail in both the darkest and lightest areas. This is demonstrated by the way the graph starts at the lower left axis and ends by sloping downward to the bottom right axis. Despite the spike on the left side, the distribution of tones is relatively even across the graph. Photo © Kevin Kopp

A perfectly exposed image will (generally) look like a bell curve, with most of the information in the center of the histogram, and tapering amounts in the edges. This is of course an over-simplification. Specular highlights (bright light reflections) that are perfectly fine can cause spikes and a photograph of a subject that's generally light or dark to begin with will affect what range of the histogram data you see. The best way to get used to using the histogram data is to review lots of images in this mode, after a short time the data here will become an invaluable tool for evaluating your images.

It's important to be aware of the overall brightness of your subject, and what sort of detail you'd like to capture. No current digital camera can completely capture every range of light from the darkest shadow to the brightest highlight, and so it's necessary to pick what part of the image needs the most detail and focus on that "dynamic range." If, for example, you're photographing the embroidery of a bride's wedding dress, be sure that the histogram curve extends all the way to the right edge of the graph (otherwise you've got overexposure in your image and the detail won't come out). On the other hand, if you're trying to capture detail in the dark tuxedo of a groomsman, it might be more important that the left side of the histogram curve reach the edge of the graph.

The RGB histograms are even more detailed, they indicate if any of the individual colors in the scene are too bright or too dark. If the histogram for a color is weighted to the left then the color is not as dominant in the scene. If it's too far to the right, information for that color will be missing in the image.

Highlight and Shadow Alerts

The other handy image-review modes are the highlight alert and the shadow alert, which are also accessed by pressing the Info button repeatedly. In the highlight alert, the camera flashes areas of the image that are overexposed, while in the shadow alert (the feature not often found on digital cameras) the camera flashes portions of the image with underexposure.

All of these modes, when used during shooting, can help judge the exposure of your image (even more accurately than the plain LCD playback can) and can often be used to help figure out what settings or compositional needs should be changed to result in a properly exposed image.

On Shutters and Apertures

Before we go into the shooting modes, here's a quick primer on the way that shutter speed and aperture work together to create an image. When light enters the camera through the lens, it has to pass through two different gateways before it strikes the sensor, and the settings of those gateways determine whether or not the photograph comes out correctly exposed. The aperture and the shutter, these two mechanical openings allow and prevent light from entering the camera.

The aperture is an iris opening located inside the lens. This opens or closes as instructed by the camera and the position of the blades is called the aperture's f/stop. Each time the iris is opened a stop, the amount of light entering the camera doubles. Each time the aperture is closed a stop, the amount halves. Aperture values are expressed as numerical settings that don't exactly seem to double, but despite the numbers the light entering the camera follows the doubling progression. Common settings are f/2.8, f/5.6, f/8, f/16, f/22 and so on. Even more confusingly, f/2.8 is said to be more "open" while f/22 is said to be more "closed" because these numbers are really ratios. When the camera is set to f/2.8, the blades of the internal aperture are wide apart which results in a "wide" hole, when they are at f/22 they are close together which results in a "closed" hole. (Photographers will often say that they are stopping "down" toward f/22 and stopping "up" toward f/2.8.)

Not only does the aperture setting control the amount of light entering the camera, but it also effects the way the image looks because it controls what's called "depth of field," which can be thought of as the amount of acceptable sharpness in the image. The other main things that affect depth of field are the focused distance and the focal length in use.

Let's say we set up a vase of flowers just a few feet in front of the camera with a person standing a few feet behind the flowers, between the vase and a mountain range behind the vase. When the aperture is set to f/2.8 and we focus on the flowers in the vase, only those flowers will be in focus. The person behind the vase and the mountains will appear blurry. Instead, if we set the aperture to f/8 and focus again on the flowers, we might get the flowers in focus and the person is somewhat sharp, but the mountain in the background would still be a blur. Finally we set the camera to f/22 and all three are acceptably sharp.

Changing things around a bit, we focus on the person and set the camera to f/2.8. Now the flowers and the mountain are blurry but the person is in focus. Setting the camera to f/8 we get the flowers and the person in sharp focus and the mountain blurry, and as would be expected we see all of them in focus at f/22.

Why does this happen? When the blades of the aperture iris are wide open (at 2.8) they allow light to enter the camera from a variety of angles, which means that light coming from far away subjects is striking the sensor on several different places, and this causes lack of sharpness. When the aperture iris is closed down, only light that's in a parallel line from the subject can enter the camera, and so all the light hits the sensor at the same place, and it's all in focus.

That's not the only thing going on inside the camera though, there's also a shutter, a mechanical device, which consists of curtains that open and close across the focal plane, controlling how long light strikes the sensor.

The aperture opens and closes to change the depth-of-field, but the result is that the incoming light doubles or halves every time you open up or close down the aperture, respectively. So the shutter needs to balance that out.

Going back to our vase, let's say we set the camera to f/2.8 and focus on the flowers. The camera's metering system determines that it needs to let in 1/500th of a second worth of light to make a properly exposed picture. Now we stop down (close the aperture) one stop to f/5.6, which halves the light. Since we now have half as much light, we need to leave the shutter open for twice as long, and the result is a shutter speed that is 1/250th of a second. The E-510 has shutter speeds from 60 seconds to 1/4000th of a second, which makes it able to handle a variety of shooting needs.

Many photographers just leave their cameras on the auto modes, (which we'll talk about below) but then they miss out on the creative possibilities of selecting their own shutter speeds, aperture settings or doing it all manually by setting both. Sure the camera often picks great shots, but it's a lot better when the photographer gets to pick whether the mountain in the background is in focus or not.

Shooting Modes

The majority of SLR cameras ever made share a number of similar shooting or exposure modes, and the E-510 is no exception. Often referred to as "priority" modes, allow one or more camera functions to be controlled by the photographer, while letting the camera select the corresponding settings to make a proper exposure. For example, in Aperture Priority mode, the user sets the desired aperture setting and the camera then picks the shutter speed necessary to achieve a correct exposure (according to the selected metering mode).

The E-510 also has a "Program" mode that's part of the basic shooting mode that picks the optimum shutter speed and aperture based on the lighting at hand, which is a great mode for the beginner photographer, and an equally great mode when a quick and important subject happens in front of the camera. Simply put the camera in the Program mode and capture the image, then go back and change to another mode to get more creative control on subsequent shots. (An AUTO mode is also available on the E-510 which works similarly to Program mode, but will automatically trigger the pop-up flash in low light.)

By contrast, the built in "picture modes" allow the photographer to tell the camera what sort of scene is being captured, and the camera then changes the settings to suit that sort of subject.

The top Mode dial on the E-510 is used to set the camera in any of the four basic modes, in the AUTO mode, or in one of five picture modes. There's also an additional "Scene" setting SCENE setting that activates the camera's rear menu system and provides access to the five picture settings on the Mode dial, plus an additional 13 picture scenes.

This can be a bit confusing; after all it means that there are two different ways to set the main picture scenes, either by dialing in the setting on the Mode dial, or by putting the mode dial on the "scene" setting and using the arrow keys to select the picture mode. Still, it's faster to dial in the picture modes on the top dials than to select them from the menu so it's handy to have the most common picture modes on the top of the camera.

Each picture mode is designed to help tackle a tricky photographic scene and they can be quite handy in a number of photographic pinches and so it's handy to know what they do, while the basic modes are the staple of photography and so it's important to know what they all do in order to get the most out of shooting with the E-510.

Program Mode P

This setting instructs the camera to set both the shutter speed and the aperture by itself with very little (if any) interaction from the photographer. Generally the E-510 (and most cameras) does a decent job picking the right combination of settings.

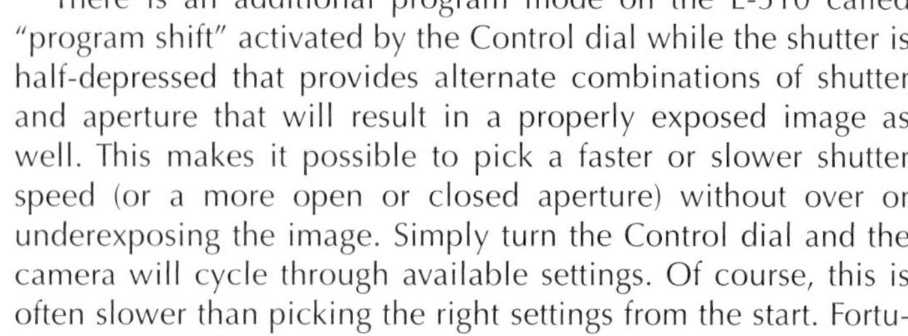

There is an additional program mode on the E-510 called "program shift" activated by the Control dial while the shutter is half-depressed that provides alternate combinations of shutter and aperture that will result in a properly exposed image as well. This makes it possible to pick a faster or slower shutter speed (or a more open or closed aperture) without over or underexposing the image. Simply turn the Control dial and the camera will cycle through available settings. Of course, this is often slower than picking the right settings from the start. Fortunately that's why there are additional basic modes.

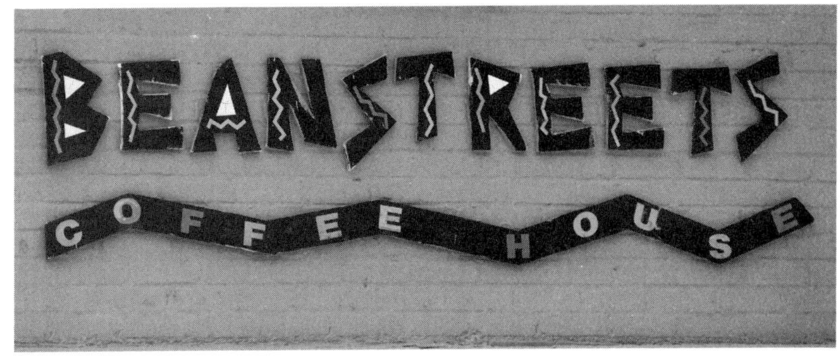

The Program mode picks both shutter speed and aperture for correct exposure. However, the combination of the two can be adjusted while maintaining the equivalent exposure using Program shift. Just turn the Control dial while partially depressing the shutter release and the camera will pick a new combination. Photo ©Kevin Kopp

Aperture Priority A

Using the Control dial to set the desired aperture, the camera picks the appropriate shutter speed. With this setting the photographer can set a fixed aperture to control depth of field (to blur the background or to ensure that all parts of a photo are in focus) and then the camera picks the matching shutter speed. This is a great setting for capturing images where the depth-of-field is important but it requires a watchful eye over the automatically selected shutter speed to make sure that your subjects won't suffer from motion blur.

Shutter Priority S

Using the Control dial to set the desired shutter speed, the camera picks the appropriate aperture. With this mode the shutter speed is selected, useful for stopping the action in a sporting event or forcing a slow shutter speed to introduce blur into an image for creative reasons. Since the shutter speed is selected by the photographer, it's good to be sure the chosen selection doesn't result in a picture with a depth-of-field different than intended.

Manual M

The photographer sets both the shutter speed and the aperture. Shutter speed is controlled via the Control dial while the aperture is set by holding down the exposure compensation button and turning the Control dial. The internal viewfinder display and the rear menu indicate the difference between the camera's settings and the exposure calculated by the camera. On the rear menu this is displayed with a bar with stop-scales on it, and a thick line indicating where the camera's set exposure lies. In the viewfinder the difference is displayed via a numerical readout of the exposure value difference and a plus or minus sign to indicate if the settings are over or underexposed from the camera's readings.

AUTO AUTO

Sets the camera to the same mode as the Program mode, but enables the built-in flash to fire in the case of low light.

On-Dial Picture Modes

Portrait : Picks settings appropriate for taking a portrait (flash pops up and fires automatically in low light.

Landscape : Useful for landscapes, sets an appropriate aperture and enhances the reproduction of blues and greens (flash does not fire automatically).

Macro : Picks settings appropriate for close-up photography (flash fires automatically in low light conditions).

Sport : Picks a fast shutter speed to avoid blur in fast moving scenes.

Night+Portrait : Picks a slow shutter speed but also triggers the built-in flash to fire (flash fires automatically).

In-Menu Picture modes

Landscape+Portrait : Sets aperture to capture both foreground and background in focus, enhances blues and greens.

Night Scene : Picks a slow shutter speed for capturing night images.

Children : Similar settings to sports.

High Key HI : Enhances bright areas in the image.

Low Key LOW : Enhances dark areas in the image.

Dis Mode : Reduces motion blur when moving the camera.
Nature Macro : Best for small, close up objects.
Candle : Enhances the reproduction of warm tones.
Sunset : Vivid reproduction of reds and yellows.
Fireworks : Slow shutter speed, similar to night scene.
Documents : Enhances the contrast between light and dark elements.
Panorama : This unique picture mode enables stitching together of images, but it requires an xD card to function.
Beach & Snow : Changes the metering to better evaluate exposures against bright backgrounds.

TIP: If you don't want the flash to fire automatically in the various scene modes, set <AUTO POP UP> to <OFF> in the menu (see page 78).

Exposure Compensation

Because there's no such thing as a perfect exposure meter, modern cameras have an adjustment dial called exposure compensation that can help perfect a shot. This is particularly helpful in the semi-automatic shooting modes of Aperture and Shutter Priority, because they allow the shooter to adjust the settings without having to switch to Manual mode.

Let's go back to our previous example of the flower vase, person and mountain. In this case we take a photograph of the subject (the person) using Aperture Priority mode because we want to set the camera to f/5 in order to leave the mountains blurry but be sure that we have enough depth-of-field to get the whole face in focus. Let's suppose the camera set the shutter speed to 1/250th of a second. Reviewing the image though we see that our shot is a little underexposed, in this case by about a full stop. Maybe it was the light in the background that threw off the meter, or maybe it was the brightness of the subject's shirt. Regardless, in order to correct this we'd normally have to switch to Manual mode and to get the same depth of field we'd dial in f/5.6 at 1/125th in order to leave the shutter open longer.

That's fine, but it requires a change of the basic shooting mode and the adjustment of at least two dials to program into the camera.

Instead, it's possible to press the exposure compensation button and dial in a change to the Aperture Priority setting, in this case we'd turn the dial until the viewfinder display or the rear LCD menu indicated that we were at +1.0. That means that we've added one stop to the camera's Aperture Priority setting. Exposure compensation can be added in 1/3 stop increments up to five stops, and it can be used to significantly change the look of an image.

Exposure compensation is probably the most powerful camera feature that's not understood by most photographers. Having the ability to adjust your image settings without having to head to the Manual mode is a tremendous advantage.

Auto Exposure Bracketing

Sometimes it's valuable to use the camera's built-in metering as a staring point, but still venture outside its suggested exposure settings in order to get a perfect picture. It's possible to use the exposure compensation settings (above) to dial in repeated changes to the exposure settings, pressing the shutter release button occasionally as you go, but it's a lot easier to use auto exposure bracketing and let the camera do that for you. The idea's really very simple; AE bracketing allows the camera to take a series of pictures.

The technical term for the stops on the exposure compensation control is EV (exposure value) and it's used throughout the discussion of camera specifications. Instead of saying "the E-510 can provide 10 stops of exposure compensation in either direction" it's possible to just say, "The E-510 provides 10 EV correction through exposure compensation." This is also the abbreviation used in the menu settings for the AE bracketing system (see page

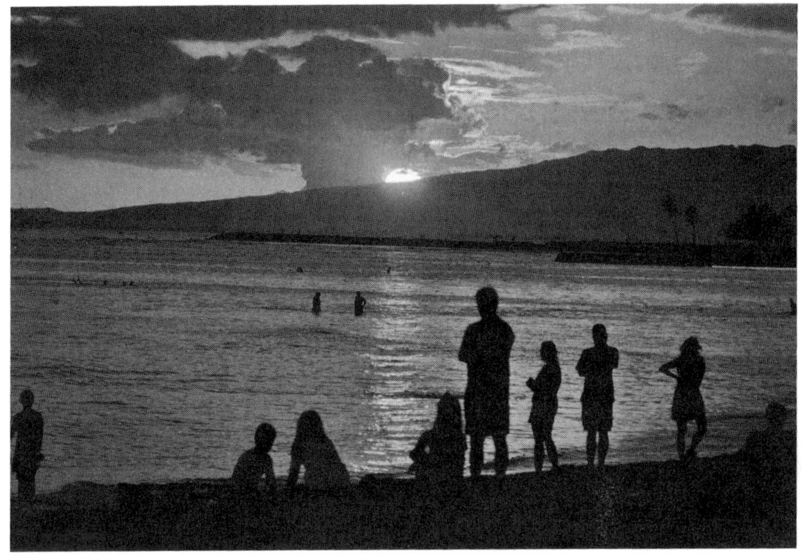

When you want to make sure that a tricky exposure is right for your creative vision, use exposure bracketing. The camera will automatically take a three shot burst with slightly different exposures. Photo © M. Schamus

75) and the E-510 can be set to perform a three shot burst at either .3 EV, .7EV or 1.Ev (or in other words, 1/3 stop, 2/3 stop, or a full stop).

The camera starts the bracket at what it considers to be the "correct" exposure and then takes a shot on either side of that exposure in a three shot burst. This setting needs to be enabled in the camera's menu system and then it is activated by simply pressing the shutter release button in single shot mode or holding down the shutter release in sequential shooting mode.

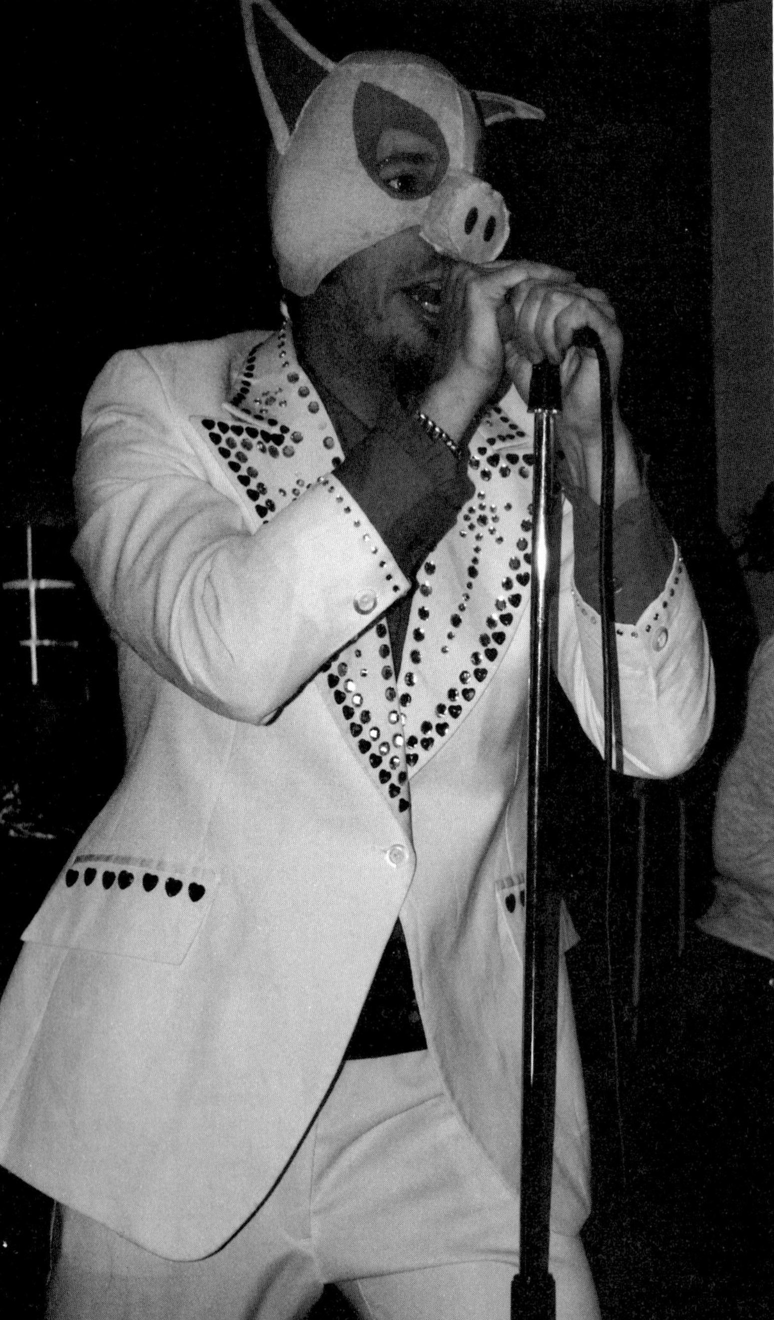

Using Flash

Many photographers think of a camera's flash as simply a tool for illuminating a dark scene. But flash is a powerful creative tool, and is fundamentally important in photography. Because many see flash photography as an "all or none" proposition (either the flash unit is on and firing full power or it is off), and because the light from a flash (either built-in or external) is often harsh and overpowering, many use the flash only as a last-ditch method of augmenting exposure.

But the flash—whether it is the camera's built-in, pop-up unit or an external system—can be a tool for enhancing the look of an image. By combining an Olympus flash with an off-camera flash cable (part FL-CB05), it's possible to move the flash away from the camera in order to get more pleasing results.

The E-510's built in flash will automatically pop up and activate in a number of the picture modes, freeing the photographer from having to think about activating the strobe. (This can be disabled via the camera's menu system, see page 78.) By default, the strobe will not activate during shooting in the basic modes. Simply pressing the flash button ⚡ found on the upper left corner of the top panel of the camera will pop up the flash in the basic modes and activate the internal flash system.

⇦ ***The Evolt E-510's built-in flash is very handy for lighting dark scenes. Just make sure the distance between the camera and the subject isn't too great. Photo © Rob Helmkamp***

Flash Basics

While the Evolt E-510 offers many sophisticated automatic flash features, it never hurts to understand what is happening when flash is used in photography. Here is a brief overview of some of the main principles of flash photography.

The Inverse Square Law

Illumination from a light source is inversely proportional to the square of the distance from the source. Thus, the light emitted by a flash unit is reduced in quantity as it travels away from the source and the brighter a light source, the greater the distance that it will illuminate.

As a formula, the Inverse Square Law is stated:

$$\textbf{Light intensity} = 1 / \textbf{Distance}^2$$

Practically, this means, if you double the distance between the flash and the subject, the flash must emit four times as much light to maintain the same level of exposure.

Distance Makes a Big Difference!

Distance	1x	2x	3x	4x	5x
Quantity of light	1	1/4	1/9	1/16	1/25

Color Temperature

The color temperature of electronic flash approximates the color temperature of daylight (often slightly cooler, about 6000k). Thus, electronic flash can be mixed with daylight for use in fill flash to reduce contrast outdoors.

Guide Numbers

Guide numbers express the relationship between output, distance, and ISO and are used in manual flash exposure to calculate the correct lens aperture at a given distance. Guide numbers are usually expressed in terms of ISO 100 and reference either meters or feet. Thus, metric guide numbers are 3.3 times lower than the equivalent guide number expressed in feet. Since today's auto flashes calculate exposure automatically, guide numbers are mainly used to quantify the output of a flash for comparison purposes.

Guide Numbers and Flash Selection: Flash output is stated in terms of its guide number (GN), which is a measurement of the amount of light emitted at a given f/stop. These numbers are usually based on ISO 100 (GN will also list the ISO that it's measured at) and a higher GN indicates a more powerful strobe. (The built-in flash in the E-510 has a GN of 39 (ft.) 12(m) at ISO 100.) When comparing flash units make sure you are comparing guide numbers in the same unit of measurement.

Digital TTL Flash

Digital TTL flash systems feature a new level of flash metering sophistication, and the Evolt E-510's flash technology is no exception. In combination with an Olympus dedicated flash unit, it measures and evaluates the subject through a series of preflashes, which are fired instantaneously before the main flash output. The preflashes fired by the E-510's flash system supply the camera's exposure system with the data about subject distance, position, reflectivity, etc. that it needs in order to create an excellent flash photograph.

Flash Modes and Techniques

There are many ways that the flash can be used to improve the photograph. Many of these techniques are fairly easy to apply. Digital photography takes the guesswork out of using flash because the photo can be viewed immediately in the LCD and, if results aren't right, the flash can be adjusted while still on scene.

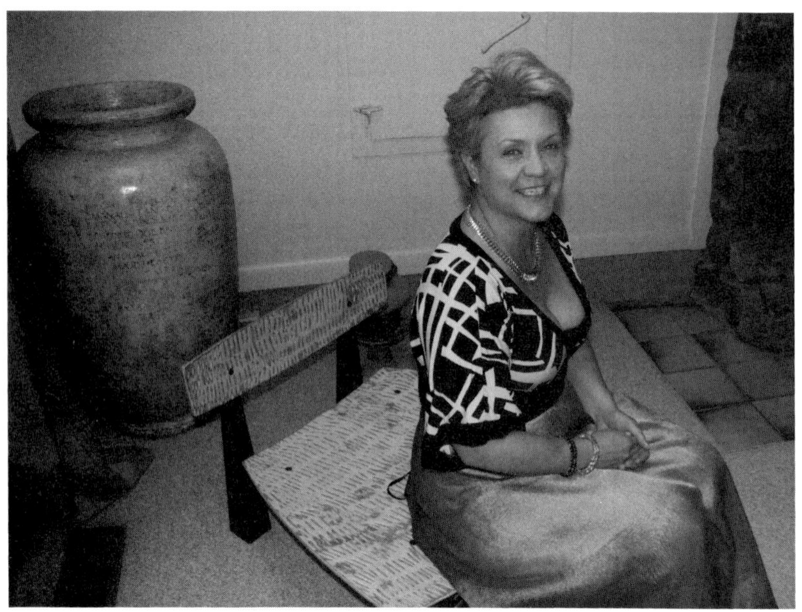

When shooting interior portraits try metering for the ambient light in the room (in this case large windows and skylights) and fill in with flash. You will often get more pleasing results than if you use flash as the main light source. Photo © Kara Helmkamp

Fill Flash ⚡

This technique uses the on-camera or an accessory flash unit to provide lighting to a subject to supplement or enhance the available light. Fill flash photography is particularly useful when photographing a subject set against a bright background where conventional exposure would result in an underexposed image and adjusting the exposure for the subject will result in an underexposed background. By activating the built-in or eternal flash it's possible to take a photograph where the lighting between the background and foreground are more similar, resulting in greater detail across the image. Fill flash is also useful in outdoor portrait photography because it lowers contrast and eliminates harsh shadows on the subject's face. Nature photographers often use it to intensify colors, which would otherwise be washed out by high-contrast outdoor shooting situations.

To get the best results, most photographers dial-down the strobe's power to maintain natural-looking lighting effect. Generally the fill light from the flash should be less bright than the ambient light. The flash output can be adjusted via second shooting menu [icon] under the flash compensation setting [icon] . The flash can be set between two stops under standard full power to two stops over full power.

Flash Synchronization Options

With cameras, such as the Evolt E-510, which have a focal-plane shutter, the flash must be fired when the shutter is open across the entire frame. The fastest speed at which this occurs is called "the flash sync speed." When an exposure with flash is made at or below the flash sync speed, the whole sensor surface will be exposed at one time. If you set a shutter speed that's higher than the maximum flash sync speed, and the flash is activated, the camera will override the setting to prevent a partially exposed flash picture.

Slow sync: Generally the camera uses the fastest possible sync speed available, but by setting slow sync the camera will use much slower shutter speeds, allowing the background exposure to register. Subjects should not move or a blur will be recorded around the frozen flash exposure (since the shutter is open longer in this mode), but the result is often pleasing. It is an effect that is in vogue right now and, thus, used in many magazine and advertising photos.

First-Curtain Sync ⚡SLOW : Used for normal flash photography, this mode times the firing of the flash as soon as the first shutter curtain uncovers the total frame. (Also called "front curtain sync.")

Second-Curtain Sync ⚡SLOW2: This is generally used with slow shutter speeds (under 1/15 second), when it is desirable for motion blur to follow a moving subject for a realistic rendition of movement. In this mode the flash is fired right before the second shutter curtain closes and covers the frame. This freezes the subject last, after the motion trail travels across the frame, so that motion blur in the finished photograph follows the object, which is how our brain perceives it should be. Also called, "rear curtain sync," it is one of the more creative uses of a camera's flash as it creates interesting effects especially from moving objects with light sources like cars or planes. Experiment with this mode to see what sort of creative images it can provide.

FP High Speed Sync: Used when higher shutter speeds or strobe motion effects are required. Some Olympus accessory flashes offer this feature (also called stroboscopic flash). This mode allows flash to be used with shutter speeds that are higher than the flash sync speed. This is possible because the flash rapidly pulses for the whole time that the shutter slit is passing across the film. This mode operates with reduced output, or power, and is most useful with relatively close subjects, or with higher ISOs.

Red-eye Reduction

Very specific conditions must occur for red-eye to be seen: a high-intensity light directed straight at the retina, and a line of sight at, or very close to, the same axis as the light that's reflected. Unfortunately, using direct flash often satisfies these conditions, especially when using small on-board flash units, which are in close proximity to the lens.

The E-510's Red-eye mode reduces this condition by firing a series of preflashes that constricts the pupils of the subject's eyes before the main flash goes off.

Other Ways to Eliminate Red-eye

If the preflash system isn't sufficient or the preflashes disturb the subject, try these other methods to reduce red-eye:

1. Take the flash off the camera.
2. Increase the level of the ambient illumination (turn up room lights), which will cause people's pupils to constrict.
3. Ask your subject(s) to look off slightly from the central axis of the lens.
4. Bounce the flash.

Off-Camera Flash

By connecting the Olympus flash unit to the camera via an off-camera cable (part FL-CB05), it's possible to create photos where the lighting does not come from directly above the camera. This makes the light more pleasing and natural looking. Flash units can also be placed in various parts or the scene or hidden underneath objects to help light a scene in a way that highlights its appearance. This is great especially in architectural or interior photography where it's possible to light trim work, statues, and archways using off-camera strobes.

This is also a great tool for macro and close-up photography as it allows the flash to be positioned away from the camera and moved at different distances or angles to the subject in order to provide a more flattering light.

Olympus also offers a PC cable adapter that fits in the hot shoe of the E-510, which provides a PC receptacle, not otherwise available on the E-510. PC cords have long been the dominant connector for studio lighting setups, and the PC adapter allows the E-510 to control an infinite array of pro lighting products.

Bounce Flash

Bouncing light off a surface diffuses the reflected light—the more irregular the surface, the more the light will be diffused. Because diffused light is less directional, it tends to wrap itself around any object in its path, so that the edges of shadows appear far softer than shadows cast by a direct light source. It is important that the flash surface is neutral and not colored or there will be an adverse affect on the subject, particularly if accurate skin tones are essential. Location of the bounce surface is also important because when the light travels to the bounce surface and then to the subject, it must cover a greater distance than if it traveled straight to the subject. Remember the Inverse Square Law! Because of these challenges, many photographers use a small bounce card or other type of bounce reflector rather than bouncing flash off a wall or ceiling.

Flash with Camera Shooting Modes

As mentioned above, the flash system does not, by default, fire in all shooting modes and, must be activated manually in some modes. This is easily accomplished by simply flipping up the pop-up unit or attaching and turning on an external flash, which sends a signal to the camera indicating that the flash is active. The camera will not trigger the built-in unit if it is recharging, instead it will wait till it reaches full power before it activates. With an external flash unit, however, the camera will trigger when the shutter release is pressed, but the flash may not fire or may not release the proper output. Thus, it is important to wait until the ready light ϟ appears in the viewfinder before firing the camera.

The flash behaves differently in the various shooting modes, and it's worth discussing these differences in order to determine the best shooting mode for the desired effect:

Program Mode

When shooting with a flash in program mode it's simply necessary to turn it on, no additional adjustments are needed. The camera will pick a combination of shutter and f/stop to work in conjunction with the flash.

Shutter-Priority mode is a great choice if you want to control the rendering of ambient light without affecting the flash exposure. Shutter speeds between 60 seconds and 1/180 second will sync with the firing of the flash. Photo ©M. Morgan ⇨

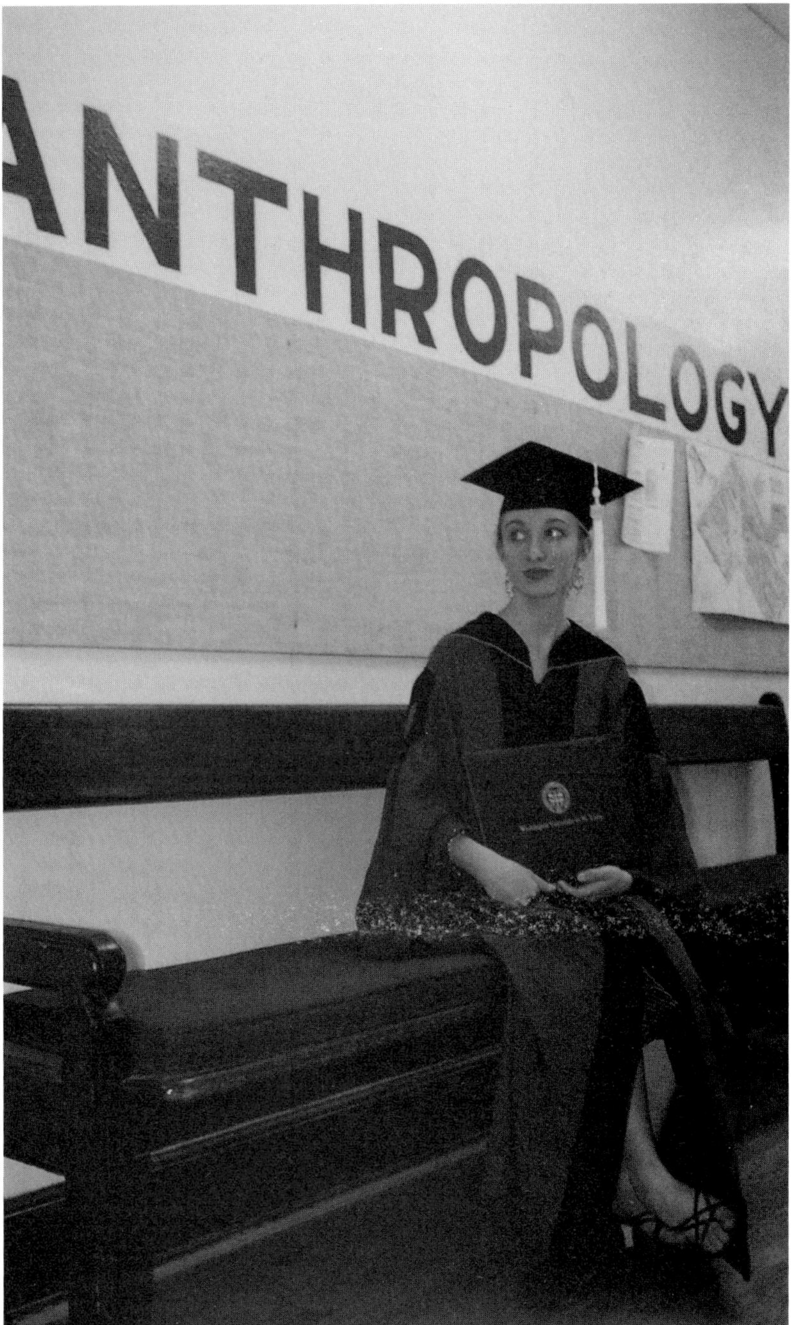

ANTHROPOLOGY

Shutter-Priority mode: Many photographers use Shutter-Priority or Manual mode with flash as it allows for precise selection of shutter sync speed, which affords control over how the background (or non-flash-lit portion of the scene) is rendered. All shutter speeds between 1/180th and 60 seconds will sync with flash. (When shooting with an FP capable Olympus strobe it is also possible to shoot up to 1/4000th of a second). If setting the camera to a slow shutter speed it's important to remember that motion blur may affect image quality of the non-flash-lit portions of the scene, even when the flash is used.

Aperture-Priority mode: In this setting the aperture is selected and the camera picks the appropriate shutter speed to match. Since the coverage of a flash unit is determined by the aperture (see page 107), selecting an f/stop changes the effective distance of the flash output. Since the camera determines shutter speed, this is the mode most likely to create an unacceptable exposure of non-flash-lit portions of the scene during flash photography.

Manual mode: This is the basic shooting mode that provides the most control as it allows for setting of both the aperture and shutter speed during flash photography. If a combination of shutter speed and aperture are chosen that would result in an under or overexposure the E-510 will provide an in-viewfinder warning. It is possible nonetheless to take a photograph in Manual mode at any aperture setting with any shutter speed from 1/180th to the maximum 1/60th.

External Flash Units

The E-510 provides automatic flash calculations for any Olympus branded strobe or any third party strobe that supports the company's TTL (through the lens) system. Connected directly to the hot shoe or externally via the FL-CB05 flash sync cord, the E-510 is able to determine the correct flash output in any of the flash's automatic modes. It's also possible for photographers to manually control the flash, but one of the best things about modern flash systems is their integration into the exposure system of the cameras, eliminating the need to perform complex flash calculations. The built-in flash exposure compensation controls on today's camera/flash systems allow the light output to be adjusted without the need for a table or slide rule.

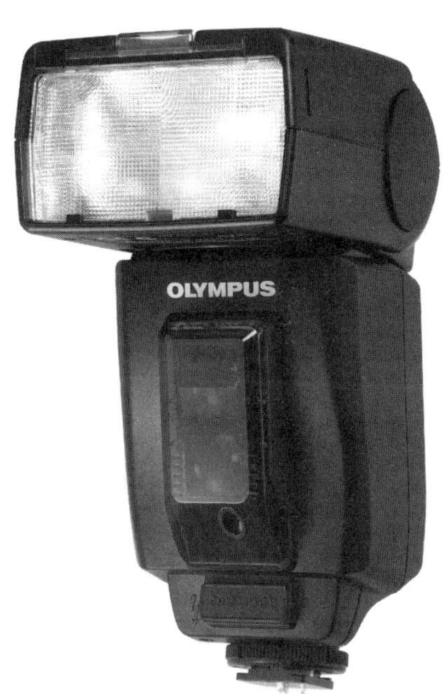

Olympus FL-50 Flash. Photo © Olympus Corporation

Olympus FL-50

The FL-50 was designed for the Olympus digital cameras, and works seamlessly with the E-510. At ISO 100 with the zoom head in the 50mm position, it provides an impressive GN of 164 (ft.) 50 (m) for truly professional lighting output. Due to the zoom flash head, the FL-50 can illuminate scenes with lenses as wide as 11mm up to telephoto lenses at 54mm. The head also swivels for bounce flash and includes a built-in wide-angle flash diffuser. The FL-50's output can be adjusted in 1/3-stop increments and includes complete manual control

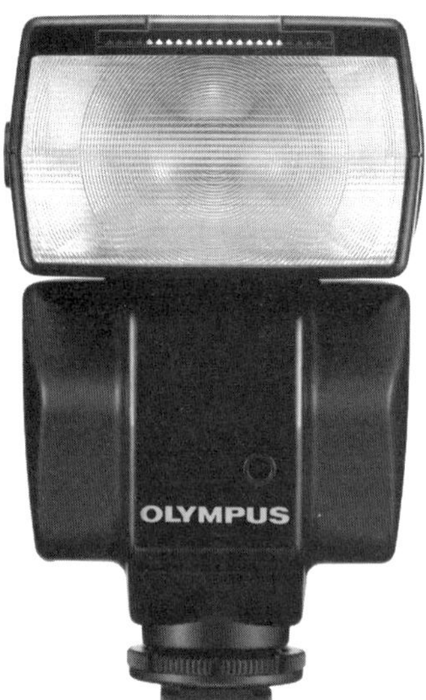

Olympus FL-36 Flash. Photo © Olympus Corporation

The FL-50 can be powered by any standard AA batteries and can also work with the company's HV-1 high-voltage power set for recycling times as fast as 1.5 seconds between shots. The built-in AF assist illuminator helps the camera focus in low light situations up to 33 feet (10 meters). This flash unit replaces the older FL-40 (which also works with the E-system).

Olympus FL-36

The FL-36 is a slightly less powerful (but more compact) sibling to the FL-50. It supplies output with an ISO 100 GN of 137 (ft.) or 36 (m) at the 42mm setting. It is also designed specifically for the Olympus E-series and works in conjunction with the E-510's TTL metering system.

The unit is 25% shorter and 35% lighter than the FL-50 and makes a nice "take anywhere" flash for photographers looking to save weight. It is powered by AA batteries, and also has a tilting and swiveling head. It replaces the older FL-20 (which also works with the E-system).

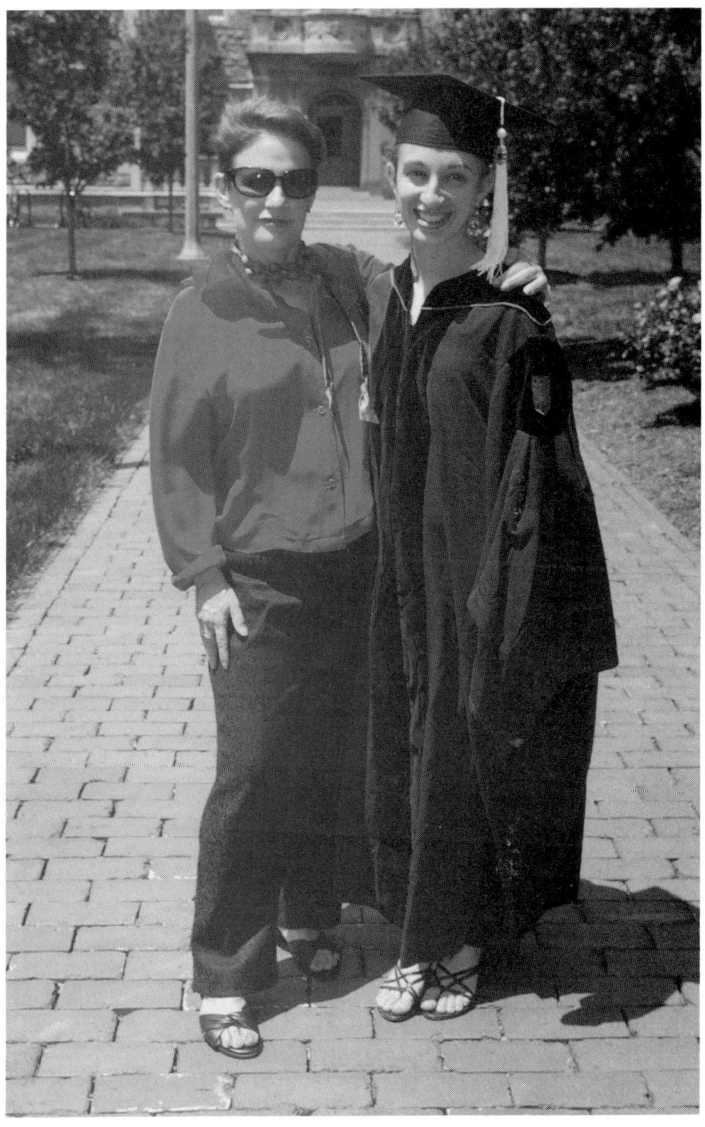

While it may seem counter-intuitive to add more light on bright sunny days, that is exactly what is needed. The flash will fill in the deep shadows, softening the light and reducing the overall contrast in the scene. Photo © M. Morgan

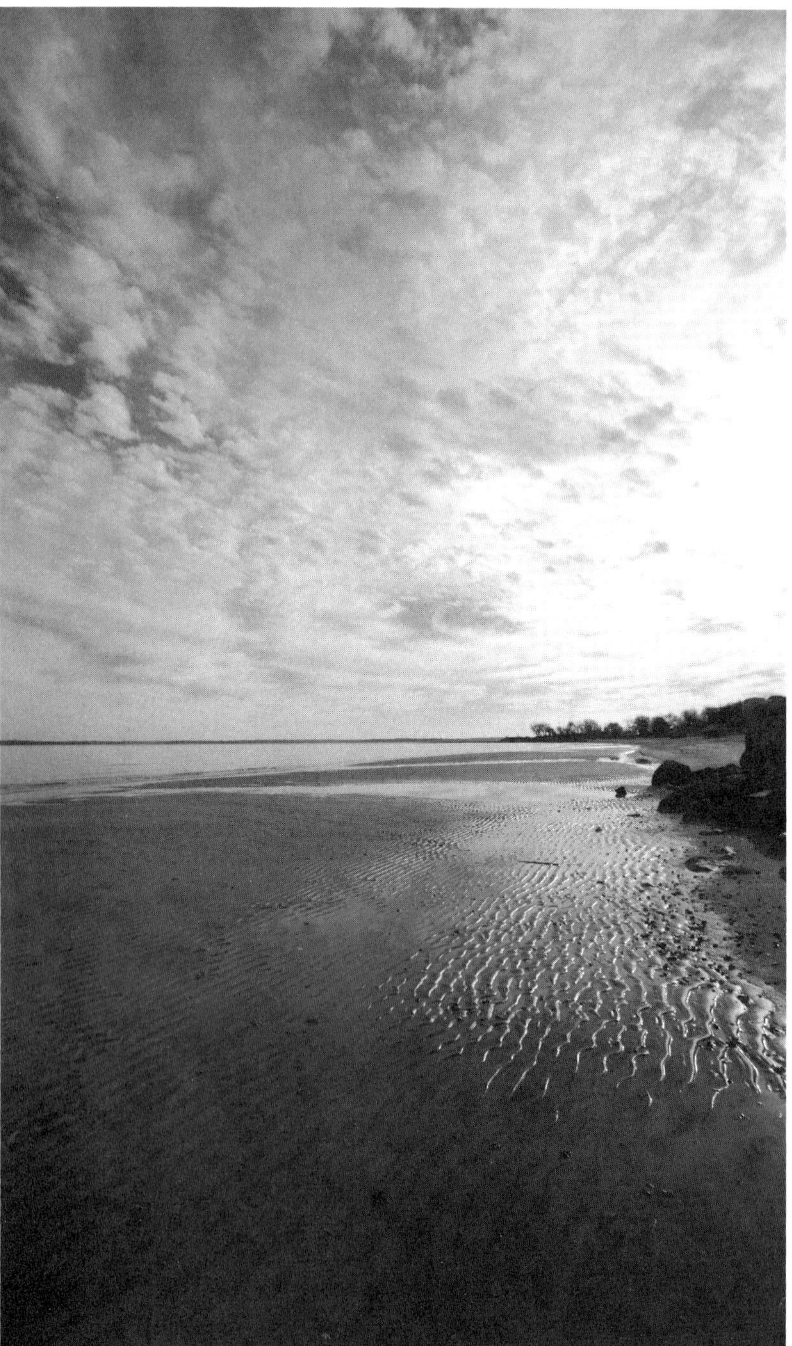

Lenses and Accessories

Olympus digital cameras are designed from the ground up to provide the highest quality image. Olympus's range of Zuiko digital lenses have a great reputation for quality and light weight, and, thus, are a nice complement to the E-510. Olympus offers its Zuiko lenses in a number of different categories. That's good because the company's original plan with the Four-Thirds system was to allow numerous manufacturers to create accessory lenses and other gear. However, early partners like Kodak and Fujifilm never got around to making four-thirds gear. A trickle of other lenses are available from Panasonic/Leica, and Sigma launched ten lenses about three months before the E-510 first shipped and since the system is open to any company, there will, no doubt, be more offerings in the future.

Choosing Lenses

There's nothing more important for the creating of images than the choice of the right lens. Even the camera takes second stage to the lens in terms of really crafting a photo. Despite the significance though, lens selection is often a difficult matter. To begin with, it's necessary to analyze the name of a lens in order to figure out what its specifications are—there's no set naming system that can help standardize the process. Many companies utilize a system of acronyms in order to denote the features and quality of their lenses.

Lens design is about tradeoffs, and there are several important ones to consider with any lens purchase. The most practical consideration of course is the focal length (or lengths) of the particular lens. A lens's focal length is simply a measurement of the distance from optical center inside the lens to the focal plane.

The quality of your image depends greatly on the lens you use. There are many options in terms of lens choice, including focal length, lens type, f/stop range, and optical construction. Some photography requires specially designed lenses, such as macro lenses for close-up photography.

Lenses tend to fall into categories, though they're loosely defined. The most traditional way to measure lenses is by their equivalent lengths in 35mm film. In that format, most people consider lenses up to around 35mm to be wide angle, 35mm to about 80mm to be standard and 80mm on up to be telephoto.

This is a bit more complicated with lenses for the E-510 because the system's lenses are listed according to their actual focal length, not that of their 35mm equivalents. (As a general rule of thumb, simply double the number on an Olympus lens to see what its view would be on a 35mm camera.) The rough guide then would be that lenses in the 7-14mm range are wide angle, 14-40mm are standard (normal range) and 40mm and higher are telephoto.

The next important specification in lens selection is the aperture range of the lens, and generally again the wider the f/stop in the lens (i.e., the lower the aperture number) the more light the lens is capable of delivering to the sensor—often called a "faster" lens. A 14mm f/3.5 would be a slower lens than a 14mm f/2.0, all else being equal.

In zoom lenses (more on those below) a lens that has the same aperture across the zoom range would generally be a higher quality lens than a comparable one with a variable f/stop (the effective speed of the lens changes as the lens is zoomed). A 7-14mm f/2.0 lens would be a better quality than a 7-14mm f/2.0-3.5, all else being equal.

But all else isn't always equal, and the third, and most difficult-to-spot lens quality is the actual optical and physical construction of the lens and its internal mechanisms, and for that it's really necessary to read the detailed description about any potential lens purchase. Again, with the Four-Thirds standard that's not much of an issue since there are so few manufacturers, but it's something to keep in mind as the system progresses.

Focal Lengths

As mentioned above, there are three main categories used when defining the focal length of a lens: normal, wide angle (or short), and telephoto (or long).

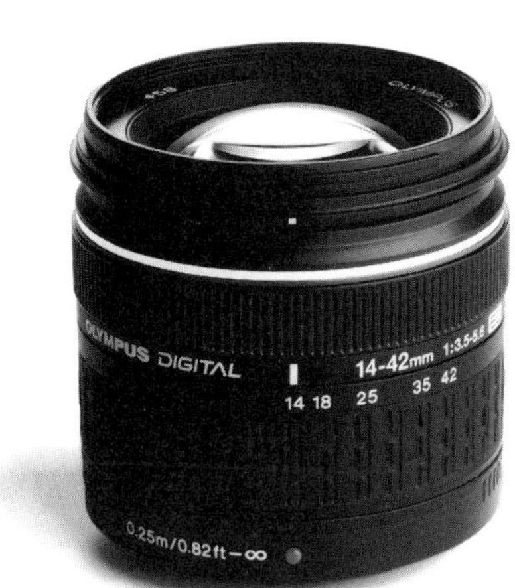

This 14-42mm lens is considered a normal lens because of the four-thirds sensor used in the Olympus E-510. It gives the same view as a typically normal lens length of the 35-80mm focal length range.

Normal Lens

A focal length lens that falls within the range of 35 – 80mm is commonly defined as a normal, or mid-range, lens. This simply means that the view of the camera captures through this type of lens is closest to how the human eye actual sees a scene. Pictures taken with these lenses usually appear "normal." Lenses are sometimes listed according to their 35mm equivalent, but Olympus lists their lenses by their actual focal length. This means that, for Olympus-supported lenses, 14 – 40mm is considered a normal length lens.

Wide-Angle Lens

A wide-angle lens is defined as any lens length that is shorter than a normal lens, or less than 35mm. (For Olympus lenses, a lens shorter than 14mm is considered wide

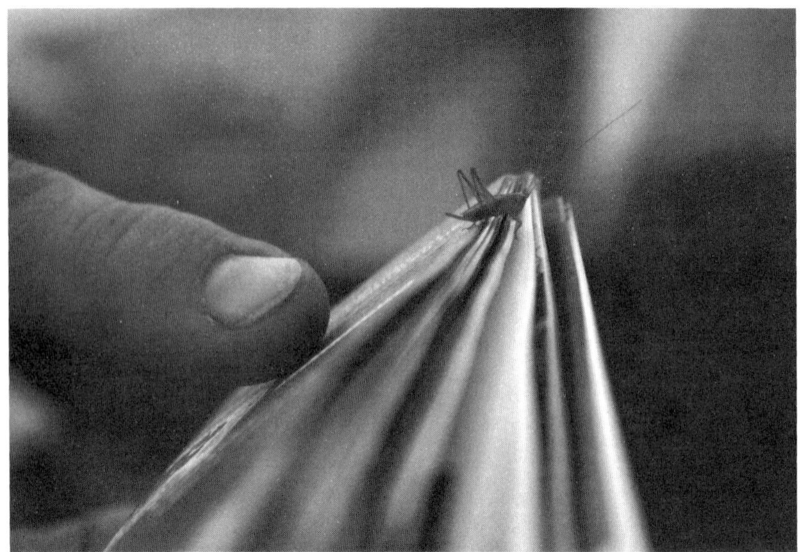

A wide-angle lens allows you to get closer to your subject than a normal focal length lens would allow, and in this image, the wide-angle view effectively isolates the subject from the rest of the image. Photo © Kara Helmkamp

angle.) Wide-angle lenses, or short lenses, pick up an increasingly wide angle of view of a scene because of the shortened focal length. For the most part, wide-angle lenses show little barrel distortion, except at the short end of the scale. As a rule of thumb, the shorter the lens, the more barrel distortion the lens creates. This means that straight lines, such as walls, look curved in an image taken with a wide-angle lens. Fish eye lenses, a subcategory of wide-angles, show the most barrel distortion because their focal lengths are the shortest of wide-angles, and are often used to create this special effect.

Wide-angle lenses allow you to get very close to the subject, offering many creative effects. The closer an object is to a wide-angle lens, the more disproportioned it appears.

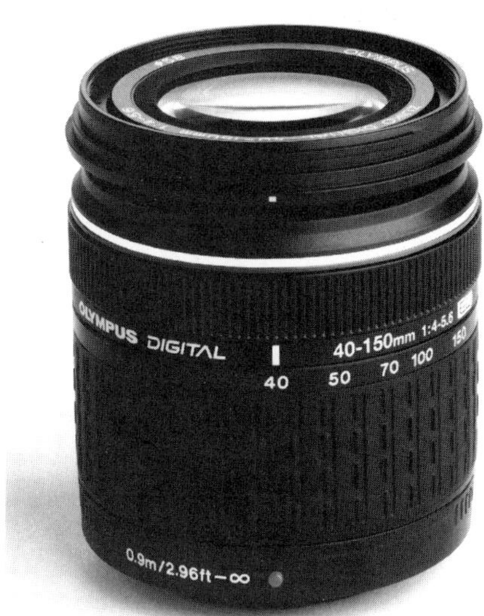

A telephoto-length lens is a good choice for any type of photography that requires the photographer to be relatively distant from the subject, such as wildlife photography. The magnification factor of the Olympus Four-Thirds system makes any focal length over 40mm a telephoto lens.

Telephoto Lens

The term "telephoto" refers to any lens that is longer than a normal length lens, or longer than 80mm. (For Olympus lenses, a lens longer than 40mm is considered telephoto.) Telephoto lenses, or long lenses, see an increasingly smaller part of the scene so that the subject is magnified in the image area. There is no barrel distortion with a telephoto lens, however a telephoto compresses a scene, making far-away objects appear closer to the subject than they actually are. Telephoto lenses also allow the photographer to be further from the subject and still capture the subject with good detail.

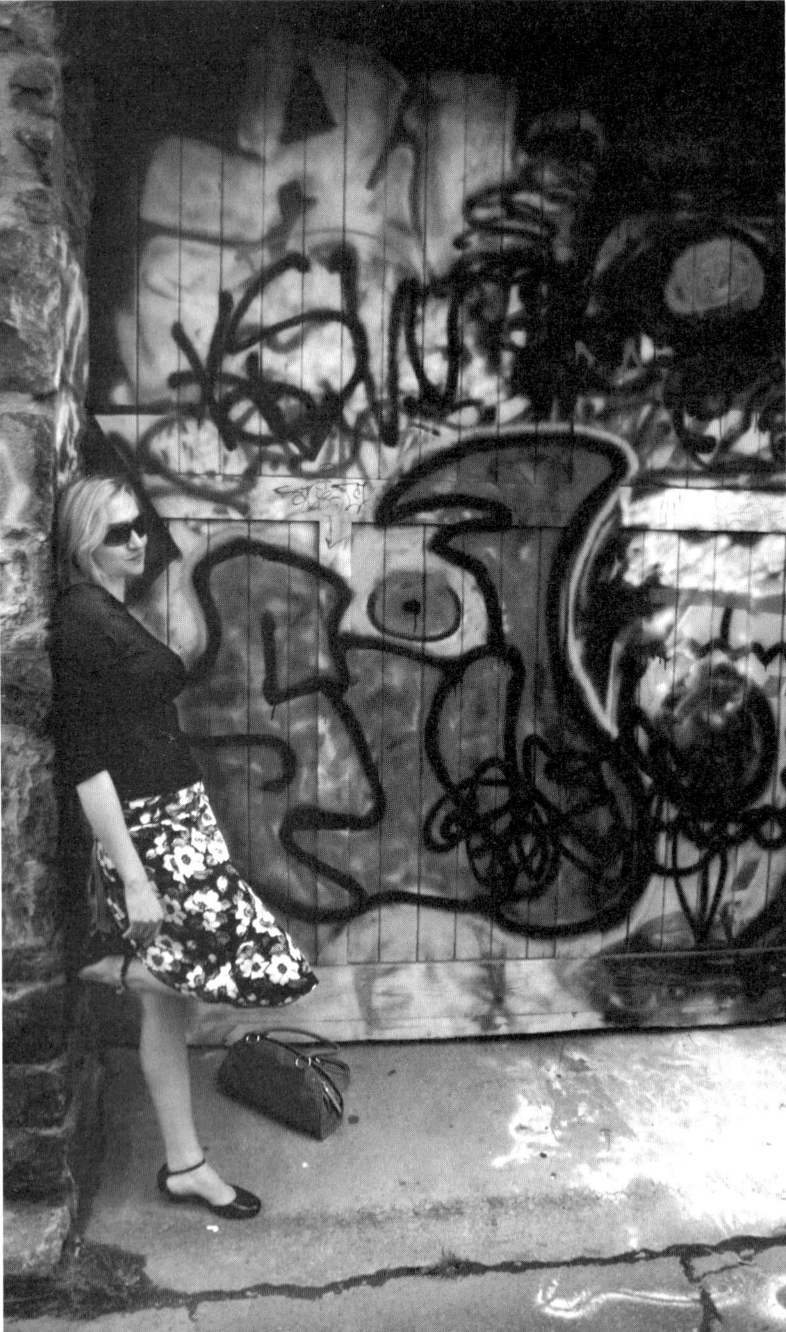

Zoom vs. Prime Lenses

There are two basic types of lenses: zoom lenses and prime lenses. A prime lens is one that has only one fixed focal length, while a zoom is one that allows for the selection of focal lengths by adjusting the lens.

When zoom lenses were introduced decades ago, there was simply no way for companies to maintain the high quality in zooms that they could in prime lenses. Too many optical compromises and moving parts made for problems in image quality. These days though with the aid of computer design and other new technology, the zoom lenses made for SLR cameras are very high quality and while a prime lens will still be a bit sharper and tend to have a better maximum aperture, zooms are optically excellent and offer much more versatility. Zoom lenses are, however, almost universally larger and heavier than their prime counterparts (though they are less than carrying several prime lenses).

Zuiko Digital Lenses

The Olympus range of lenses for the E-510 includes three tiers of lenses, those that the company considers to be "super high-grade," "high-grade," and "standard". At the time the E-510 was released (and this book was written) the company offered five lenses in each of the lineups, plus a teleconverter in the high-grade line. (A teleconveter attaches between the lens and the camera, providing additional magnification without needing to go out and spend a ton on a new longer-telephoto lens. It's a nice solution for occasional super-tele needs.)

If one lens focal length can serve a majority of your photographic needs, a prime lens is a good way to go. But if you need a variety of focal lengths, a zoom lens might better meet your needs. There are positives to both choices; the key is to discover how you prefer to shoot. Photo © Kara Helmkamp

Distinguished by a "platinum" line on the lens barrel, the super high-grade lenses are not only dust and splash proof, but also are built to meet the rugged requirements of a pro shooter. The zooms in this range were all single-aperture models and several of these primes in this selection had speeds of f/2.0.

The high-grade line included the company's fisheye lens (a lens that's so wide angle that it distorts the view tremendously, just like looking through a peephole) and a macro lens. These lenses are also dust and splash proof though they are not built with the same level of durability of the super high-grade lenses.

Zoom lenses in this product range had variable f/stops (such as f/2.8-3.5) and the only primes were the fisheye and the macro.

Finally, Olympus offered a range of standard lenses that are "developed for cost-performance and portability". The zooms in this class tended to go from f/3.5-6.3 and the range includes a 35mm macro.

OM Lens Use

Olympus also offers an adapter ring that allows the E-510 to accept the company's older OM lenses, of which there are dozens of models available on the used-camera market. Of course, the older OM lenses are not designed to work with a modern digital camera, so features like autofocus, metering and other settings will be disabled. But it's a nice way for Olympus aficionados to break out their old glass.

Third-Party Lenses

Around the same time as Olympus announced the E-510, several additional companies announced Four-Thirds lenses to complement not only Olympus cameras but also Four-Thirds systems from Panasonic and Leica as well. Panasonic/Leica, who uses the Four-Thirds standard on their Lumix cameras announced a new Leica branded lens. Long considered one of the most respected lens manufacturers in the world, the lens caused a commotion among Olympus shooters.

The other major producer of Four-Thirds lenses is Sigma, who also makes lenses for virtually every other camera system on the planet. At launch Sigma had announced eleven lenses, including several zooms and primes in their high-end EX DG and EX DC HSM lineup and several zooms in their lower-end DC line.

Filters

The sale of lens filters has taken a huge hit since the advent of digital. Lens filters, once the staple of the creative photographer, have fallen out of popularity because the majority of the effects for which filters were used can be achieved via software after shooting. There's no reason to add a warming filter to a lens to capture a great sunset if a simple change to the white balance or a single button in an image-processing program will achieve the same effect.

Lens filters are easy to use, and they come in two basic styles, screw-on and holder-mounted. Screw-on filters need to be the correct size for the front of the lens (this size is measured in millimeters, and is listed on the front of the lens) so it's necessary to have a filter that fits each different lens barrel size in your arsenal. Holder-based filters slide into a carrier that's in turn mounted to the front of the lens using an adapter ring. In this case, all you need to use the system on different lenses are the appropriate adapter rings.

There are a number of useful filters that should be inside every digital camera bag, and the use of these filters will cut down on editing, improve the look of images, and should be used often:

UV and Skylight Filters

These two filters do very little visually (they subtract some of the UV wavelengths from visible light, slightly clearing up an image on a hazy day) but they also provide protection for the front of a lens without degrading the quality of the image captured. These thin glass filters screw-mount to the front of a lens and protect it from scratches and other damage. For this reason alone it's worth it to put a UV or skylight filter on every lens you own.

Circular Polarizer

This is one of the few filters that's impossible to duplicate in software, and that's because a polarizer changes the way that light enters the camera. A circular polarizer is a type of polarizer that doesn't cause issues with the camera's focus and exposure system (as opposed to older linear polarizer) and should be used with autofocusing and auto exposure systems like the E-510. A circular polarizer screws onto the front of a lens and can be rotated to achieve the desired effect.

A polarizer performs several functions. When rotated up to 90° from the sun it will darken the sky, reduce glare and reflections in an image (more on this in a second), and increase saturation in an image. This effect can be dramatic and there's a night-and-day difference between a landscape shot with and without a polarizer.

The related effect is that a polarizing filter can remove the glare and reflections found on non-metallic, shiny objects. That's because the filter is actually removing light that enters the lens from certain directions and so when turned properly it can nearly completely remove reflections in things like glass, water, etc. It's particularly handy when trying to shoot through a window on a sunny day and the result will be a photograph were the other side of the glass is visible, instead of a photo with nothing more than a reflection of the photographer and whatever is behind them.

Neutral Density Filters

Neutral density filters simply reduce the amount of light entering the lens without distorting the image. This is handy in ultra-bright shooting environments where a slow shutter speed is desired, but where the ambient light would force the use of a high shutter speed to compensate for the brightness. Without a good neutral density filter there's sometimes no way to achieve the artistic effect desired.

ND filters come in handy on the beach, when shooting in snowy conditions, at midday and any time it's necessary to just reduce the light entering the camera without affecting the quality of that light. They come in a variety of strengths measured by the amount of light they reduce, such as 2x, 4x or 8x. The factor here is the same as an f/stop. A 2x filter removes two stops of light from the scene.

Graduated neutral density filters are a subset of ND filters that start clear on one side of the filter and end up being gray on the other, either in a smooth gradation or split down the middle. These filters are handy when only a portion of the incoming light is too bright (sunrise over a field, for example) but the rest of the image is less bright.

ExpoDisc

Not exactly a filter, there's a product called ExpoDisc that should probably be part of every digital photographer's arsenal as it's a great idea. Essentially ExpoDisc is a circular tool that is held in front of the lens in order to create a perfect custom white balance. The ExpoDisc scatters incoming light in much the same way that the glass-block windows often found in public bathrooms do.

The ExpoDisc is held over the lens while putting the E-510 in one-touch white balance mode and it eliminates the need to find a piece of white paper and have someone hold it for you.

Tripods and Camera Supports

No photographer should be without a good tripod, as there's no better tool available for getting good, sharp images. The number one cause of a poor photo is blur, and blur can be eliminated with the use of a good tripod. This is especially true for photographers who are shooting sports, capturing long-exposure shots, or crafting portraits or landscapes—in other words—everyone.

Sure, the E-510 has built-in image-stabilization, but in the real world of photography it's better to eliminate that motion before it gets into the camera and the best way to do that is with a tripod.

There are countless tripods available, ranging from the inexpensive models found just about everywhere a single camera is sold, all the way up to hand-assembled carbon fiber models found at the most professional-oriented camera stores. They all do the same thing, provide a support for the camera while eliminating motion. Of course, that's like saying that all cars do the same thing (drive you from point A to point B) and there are certainly reasons to carefully pick a tripod to suit your needs.

Generally the low-cost tripods found on the racks near the disposable film cameras aren't worth the $20 you'll spend on them. Poor construction translates to motion, and that's what a tripod is designed to eliminate. Likewise, a $500 tripod might be overkill for all but the most specialized photographer. Tripods are also designed for different weight camera systems so a model that's perfect for a 30 pound professional medium format camera would be overkill for a light, compact system like the E-510.

Before you buy any tripod, put your camera with your longest lens on it and set it up. See if it's easy to assemble and disassemble, if it resists motion (grab the legs and twist and shake them) and if it's light enough to carry with you. It should also have easy-to-open and easy-to-close legs, it should not feel difficult to setup and any moving parts should rotate freely and easily without forcing them. Aluminum and carbon fiber models are the most common professional models as they offer good support and low weight.

A tripod is almost a necessity for many types of photography. Low-light situations almost always require a camera stabilizer, whether that comes in the form of a tripod, a beanbag, or a doorway to prop your camera against. Photo © Kara Helmkamp 

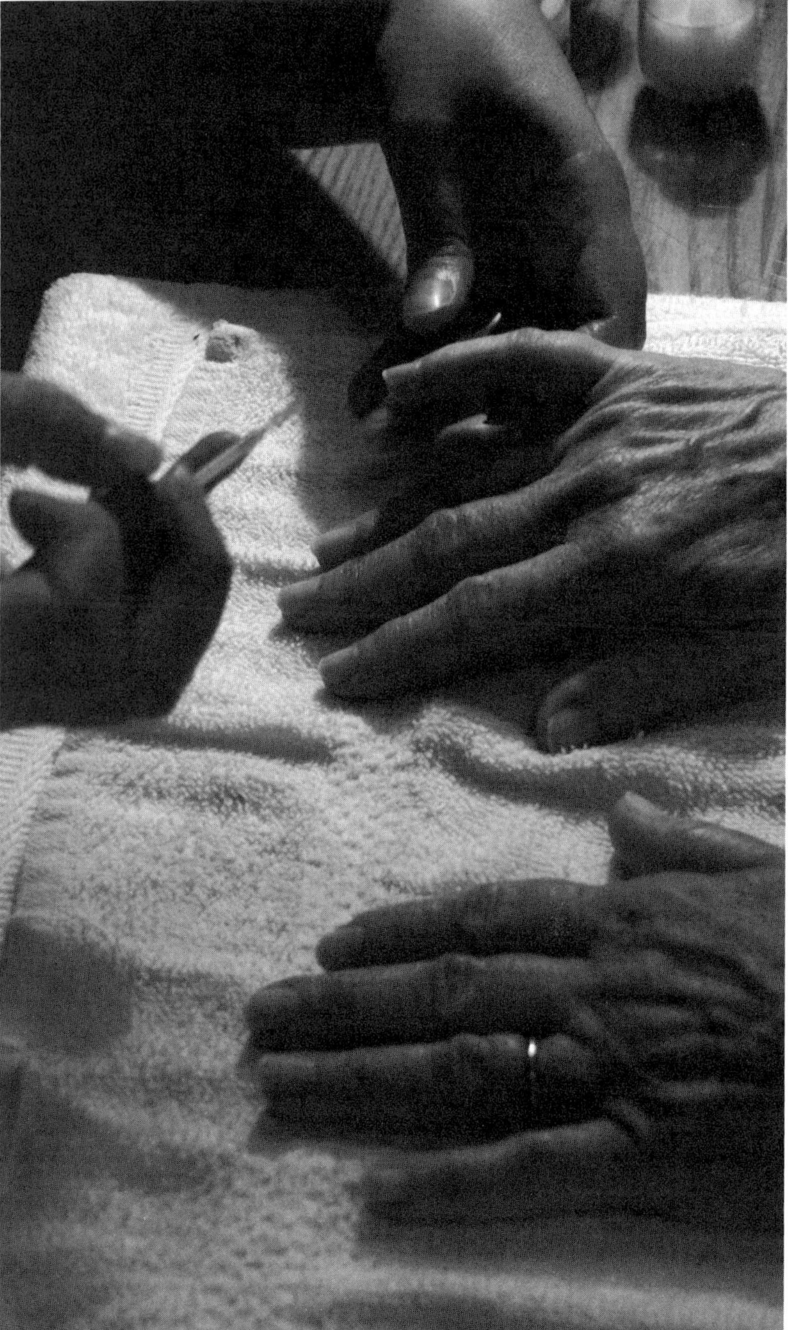

Pay attention to the "head" that comes with the tripod, as this is the interface between your camera and the support. There are many styles available from simple twist-lock ball heads to complicated trigger-grip panhead sports models. A good camera store will be able to show you various models for the types of shooting you plan to focus on. Be sure to try any camera head with your E-510 as some systems work better for some camera and shooting styles.

Cleaning Tools and Other Accessories

In order to keep cameras working properly, it's important to keep them clean and free of contaminants. The E-510 doesn't require much more than an occasional wipe-down with a dry cloth to keep it free from dust, dirt and sand but it's important to have the right materials on hand in case there's a need to clean one of the sensitive parts of the camera and lens systems.

A lens cloth and/or soft brush are the only things that should touch the glass elements on a lens (but feel free to wipe off a UV or Skylight filter with your t-shirt if you need, that's why they're on there in the first place).

The internals of the camera should only be cleaned according to Olympus's instructions, which involve the use of a bulb-blower and very careful application of puffs of air. Yes, the E-510 does automatic dust removal, but that doesn't get the dust out of the camera, it just shakes it off the sensor system. To really get a dust-free image it's necessary to clean out the camera's insides, especially after changing lenses in dusty or dirty environments.

Battery Supply

The battery in the E-510 recharges in about two-hours, which isn't a terribly long time, unless you want to take a photo while the battery is plugged into the wall. Investing in a second battery will provide wait-free shooting. When the first battery dies, simply slip in the second battery while charging the first.

Media Cards

Just as it's annoying to have to wait for your battery to recharge before using your camera again, it's equally annoying to have to wait to empty the contents of a memory card before shooting. A second (or third) card will make it much easier to continuously take photos, especially when on long trips away from the computer.

Media Storage

If you're going to shoot with more than one card, spend a few dollars on a soft-shell or hard-shell card storage case to protect your memory cards.

Photo Printers

Not exactly an accessory, nevertheless, a good-quality photo printer is a great additional investment for the E-510 shooter. Look for a printer with the words "photo" on it, preferably one that also includes the words "pro" or "professional," especially if you'd like your photos to last a lifetime.

The inexpensive printers available at office supply stores are nice, but their images don't last, and they don't showcase the high-resolution sensor in the E-510. Instead opt for a true photographic printer and you'll have images that'll last generations.

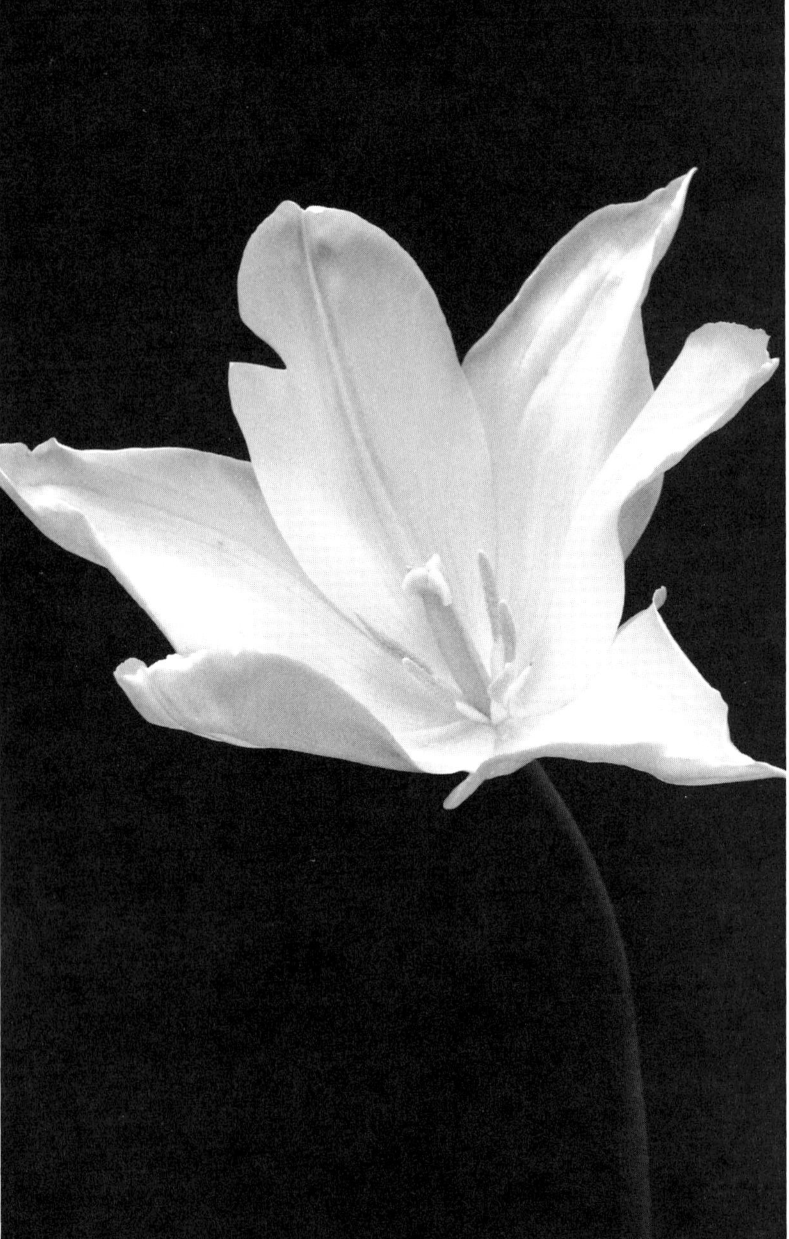

Working with Your Images

No photographer has ever woke up and said, "I can't wait to take some pictures today and show them to absolutely no one, for the rest of my life." Photography is about sharing your vision, and in order to do that, you need a way to get your images from the camera to the rest of the world.

Image Options

The two main ways to go about this are by transferring picture files to your computer (where you can edit and enhance, archive, email, and print them) or by printing them directly from the camera. Very few people choose the later route, simply because direct-printing doesn't solve the need for image storage. Direct printing is great for parties or weddings, or anytime you want to produce prints immediately, but for most purposes, it is best to copy your files to your computer (so you don't lose them). In this case, you might as well do that first and then print your images. There are a few ways to get images to your computer, and a few ways to manage and edit them once you get them there.

Direct USB Transfer vs. Card Reader

The E-510 includes a high-speed USB 2.0 port, designed to allow direct transfer of images to a computer. This port is also used for direct printing, more on that below. That means that it's possible to shoot with the E-510 and transfer images to your Mac or PC with nothing more than the USB cable that comes in the box.

You'll want to enjoy and share your photos by printing them and emailing them to friends and family. The first step, generally, is to download them into a computer using a card reader.

But there are some great advantages to using an external card reader over the connection built into the camera. The first is that the external card reader will operate faster than the built-in USB 2.0 port, even if you're using a USB 2.0 card reader. A FireWire card reader (useable if your computer has a FireWire port) is even faster for the sustained transfers of numerous images.

Using a card reader doesn't affect the battery life of your camera. Every time you connect the camera to the computer for transfer, the battery slowly drains while the images move from camera to computer. A card reader, by contrast doesn't require any external power, and the camera can be left off, preserving battery power. (Or, you can transfer images from one card while continuing to take pictures with another card.)

Since the E-510 supports both the xD format and CF, you'll need a card reader with slots for both formats if you plan to shoot both. Multi-card readers are available as inexpensively as $15. Card readers can be purchased at electronics and camera stores.

Simply connect the card reader to a USB or FireWire port on your computer (depending on the model), with the camera turned off, remove the card from the camera and insert it in the card reader. On Windows XP, Windows Vista and Mac operating systems the card will automatically mount without the need for any additional drivers, in most cases. If the card does not mount, drivers for the card reader can be found on an included CD.

When you're done transferring images (see below) be sure to eject the card. On Windows systems, right click on the card's icon and select "eject." On Mac OS X, drag the icon of the card to the Trash.

Manual Organization vs. Software

For years the only really good way of managing one's photographic library was to do it by hand. Pioneering digital photographers spent a lot of time dragging files around, creating folders and organizing their images. Luckily a number of companies have taken a look at the needs of the digital photographer and have created software to manage digital image libraries, which are becoming such an increasingly important part of everyday life. At this point, there's not really much reason to manually drag images from folder to folder, hand cataloging them, and keeping tabs on their location. It's so simple to use any of the photographic tools on the market that digital photographers can forget about the days where it took longer to organize one's photos than it took to take them.

Free Tools for Image Management

Digital photography software programs address certain needs of the photographer, and some of them focus more heavily on one area than another. By and large, most programs fit into the category of image management, image editing, or all-in-one tools.

Olympus includes its own Master Software 2 with the E-510, and it's a great free program for both Mac and PC users. It's a surprisingly powerful all-in-one tool that allows the photographer to not only manage and organize images, but allows direct editing of Olympus raw files. Master Software 2 does not, however, allow users to import and editing of raw files from other camera manufacturers, so users of other systems won't be able to edit raw files created with their cameras.

The program also has a slightly cumbersome interface with awkwardly worded dialog boxes that can get in the way of some photographic tasks. Users looking for more streamlined all-in-one programs could turn to the free Google Picassa (picassa.google.com) on Windows machines and iPhoto on the Mac (included free with all Macs). Both of these provide the same features as Master Software 2, at the same price (free) without the confusing interface.

Advanced Software

Some photographers need a bit more power than in the free programs, with either more image editing muscle, or more powerful organizational and management tools.

A new breed of software has recently emerged that provides the photographer with professional-level file management, captioning, editing and output all in a single package. Apple's Aperture and Adobe's Lightroom are great examples of this type of program. Both provide raw-centric image editing capabilities that exceed those in the free programs and they also provide the capability for seamless management of hundreds-of-thousands of images. It's possible to move files, rate them, caption them, apply keywords, plus archive, export, and print them—all with these competent all-in-one packages.

Companies like ACD Systems and iView (now part of Microsoft) also make all-in-one packages with more sophisticated tools than those found in the free programs, though not as powerful as those in Aperture and Lightroom.

For those that require more muscular image-editing abilities Adobe's venerable Photoshop (and the lower-priced but still powerful Photoshop Elements) are great tools for creative manipulation of images. Both programs go a step further than the professional all-in-one tools, allowing for some really artistic edits.

Photoshop's power is virtually limitless and countless artists use it daily to create photographic effects that could never have been achieved with a traditional darkroom. These are also great tools to use for creating web graphics, animation and more.

Regardless of the tool used, it's important to pick an application that's able to work with a camera's raw files. As we covered earlier, raw files contain more information than JPEG files and provide more post-processing choices for the photographer.

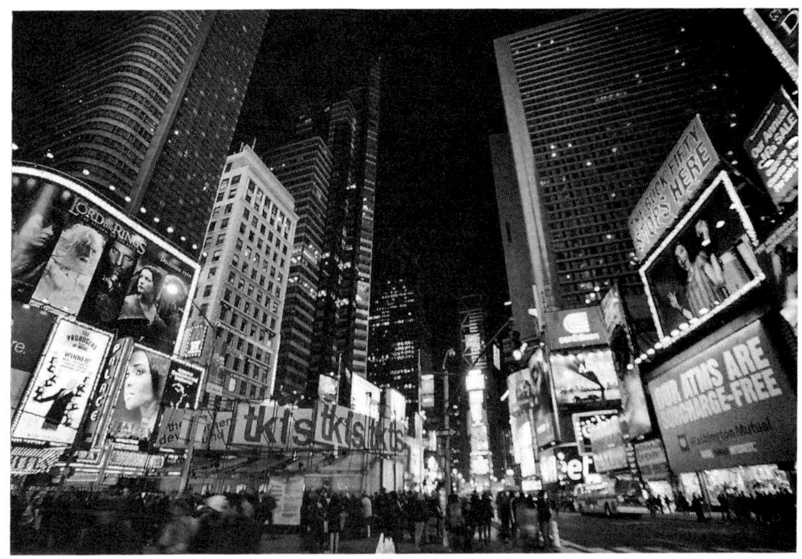

Before you know it you will have a plethora of photo files. It is essential that you devise a strategy for cataloging and backing up your photos. There are many good image management programs available on today's market, which can help you get control of your image library. Photo © M. Schamus

Storing Your Images

In some ways, digital images are more fragile than their film counterparts. This is because a digital image doesn't actually exist anywhere, it's just a collection of zeroes and ones that computer can reconstruct into the original image. Digital photographs, however, can be infinitely replicated, as long as the original data is still intact. This gives them a tremendous advantage over more traditional film in that a digital file, be it raw or JPEG can be reproduced an infinite number of times without degradation or loss.

But that requires a bit of forward thinking on the part of the photographer. It's necessary to create backups of your images in order to preserve them, and more importantly it's necessary to create backups that aren't likely to be subject to the same things that damaged the original files, should they be ruined. In other words, if your original files are damaged in a fire, any backups that are stored in the same location are likely to be damaged by the same fire. That's why professional photographers not only keep copies of their images locally, but they store them offsite as well.

There are a few ways to store copies of your images. Many photographers use inexpensive external hard drives to backup their most valuable images, purchasing drives as they go on sale at the local computer outlets and archiving copies of their work.

Hard drives are not the most durable system of archiving, since they have a large number of moving mechanical parts inside. All drives have a specification called MTBF, which stands for "mean time between failure." This is an average of how long the drive will function before it dies. Essentially, it's an expiration date of sorts spelled out for consumers.

Another backup system used by many photographers is optical media. DVDs and CDs are good for medium-term storage but the dye layer used to record the data fades over time, especially if the optical media is not stored properly. DVDs can hold 4.7GB of info at a time and dual-layer DVDs can hold twice that (but require a compatible burner that's not as common as a standard DVD drive), which makes them good secondary backup tools.

The most important thing to keep in mind though is that no one system of backup will prevent loss of files. It's important to keep a mix of drive-based and optically stored images both on site and off site. Many pro photographers keep both a collection of images on location in a fireproof safe but also ship drives and DVDs off to friends and families where they're stored in a closet or some other safe location. This gives photographers a last-ditch image recovery method should their drives fail or their studio get damaged in a disaster of some kind.

All of the image management programs provide some sort of backup tool, either through the Export or Backup command or though some other system. They allow for selected-image backups (only a few images at a time) or an en-masse export. These are terribly handy and should be used often.

Operating systems are getting into the backup game too. Starting with OS X 10.5, Mac users will be able to use a tool called Time Machine for instant restoration of deleted files, a more sophisticated version of the file recovery tools built into Windows for some time.

As Internet connections continue to get faster and faster, a new breed of online backup tools will continue to emerge and develop. Online backup is a smart way to go, as it offers the safety of offsite backups combined with the redundancy that comes when the large data centers housing these images archive them on their own, as part of their own disaster recovery efforts.

Direct Printing

The other task can easily be performed with a digital camera is direct printing. Many photographers like this as it gives them a way to go right from shooting to output without needing to take a trip through a computer.

In order to print from camera to printer it's necessary to use a PictBridge compatible model, many of which are available from all of the major manufacturers. In order to print it's simply a matter of connecting the camera and output device via USB cable and then select which images should be sent to the printer.

Every PrintBridge printer has a "standard" mode that produces a fixed kind of output, though that standard mode varies from device to device. (Some print at different paper sizes and different print settings in standard mode.) Check the

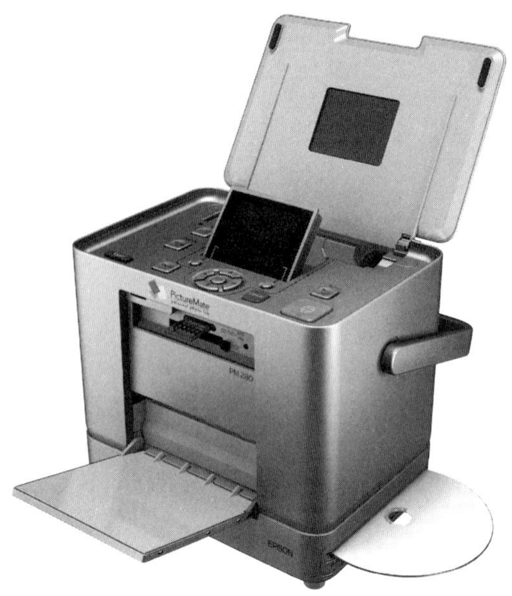

Direct printers, such as this Epson PictureMate PM 280, are great for quick, high-quality prints of events, family, and friends. This particular printer makes borderless prints, and can also burn a back-up CD. Photo © Epson America, Inc.

manual that comes with the printer to determine what sort of output will be created by printing in the standard setting.

Printing via the camera is actually very simple. Once the printer is connected, the E-510 asks for a USB setting mode (unless this is preset in the setup menus, see page 82). Simply use the arrow buttons to select Easy Print for quick printing. Once this has been selected, the camera will begin review of images on the storage card.

Use the left and right arrow keys to scroll through your images until you find one that you'd like to print. Press the print button that's located on the left corner of the top camera panel (it's the one that's used to set the shooting mode, the print icon is in green directly below the button, to the left of the viewfinder).

Pressing this button will create output using the "easy print" setting in the E-510, which outputs in the printer's standard print mode. To specify custom print settings, simply press the OK button instead, and the E-510's display will switch to a screen called <PRINT MODE SELECT>, which includes four choices. The first <PRINT> prints the selected pictures using the settings chosen in the following screens. <ALL PRINT> creates a print for every image on the card (it's a good idea to use this very sparingly). <MULTI PRINT> is used for multiple copies of an image in separate frames on a single sheet of paper, handy for things like wallet size images. <ALL INDEX> prints a contact sheet of all the images on the card. <PRINT ORDER> is used to print according to a system called print reservation, handy for selecting images to send to a printer even if one isn't connected at the time. Press OK to move to the next screen.

The next menu screen provides choices for the paper <SIZE> and <BORDERLESS> output if printing a single image, or <SIZE> and number of <PICS/SHEET> for printing multiple images. Press OK to move to the next screen.

The <PRINT INFO> screen controls whether image-shooting data like the file name and the date are printed along with the image, and the ⎙ choice specifies the number of copies to print. Press OK to move to the next screen.

Select <PRINT> to start the print job, or select cancel to exit from the printing screen. At any time during output the OK button will stop the job, bringing up a <CANCEL>or <CONTINUE> choice.

Glossary

aberration
An optical flaw in a lens that causes the image to be distorted or unclear.

angle of view
The area seen by a lens, usually measured in degrees across the diagonal of the film frame.

anti-aliasing
A technique that reduces or eliminates the jagged appearance of lines or edges in an image.

aperture
The opening in the lens that allows light to enter the camera. Aperture is usually described as an f/number. The higher the f/number, the smaller the aperture; the lower the f/number, the larger the aperture.

Aperture-Priority mode (A)
A type of automatic exposure in which you manually select the aperture and the camera automatically selects the shutter speed.

artifact
Information that is not part of the scene but appears in the image due to technology. Artifacts can occur in film or digital images and include increased grain, flare, static marks, color flaws, noise, etc.

artificial light
Usually refers to any light source that doesn't exist in nature, such as incandescent, fluorescent, and other manufactured lighting.

automatic exposure
When the camera measures light and makes the adjustments necessary to create proper image density on sensitized media.

automatic focus
When the camera automatically adjusts the lens elements to sharply render the subject.

available light
The amount of illumination at a given location that

applies to natural and artificial light sources but not those supplied specifically for photography. It is also called existing light or ambient light.

backlight
Light that projects toward the camera from behind the subject.

backup
A copy of a file or program made to ensure that, if the original is lost or damaged, the necessary information is still intact.

barrel distortion
A defect in the lens that makes straight lines curve outward away from the middle of the image.

bit
Binary digit. This is the basic unit of binary computation. *See also, byte.*

bit depth
The number of bits per pixel that determines the number of colors the image can display. Eight bits per pixel is the minimum requirement for a photo-quality color image.

bracketing
A sequence of pictures, taken manually or automatically, of the same subject but varying one or more exposure settings between each exposure.

brightness
A subjective measure of illumination. See also, luminance.

buffer
Temporarily stores data so that other programs, on the camera or the computer, can continue to run while data is in transition.

built-in flash
A flash that is permanently attached to the camera body. The built-in flash will pop up and fire in low-light situations when using the camera's automated exposure settings.

built-in meter
A light measuring device that is incorporated into the camera body.

bulb
A camera setting that allows the shutter to stay open as long as the shutter release is depressed.

byte
A single group of eight bits that is processed as one unit. *See also, bit.*

card reader
Device that connects to your computer and enables quick and easy download of images from memory card to computer.

chromatic aberration
Occurs when light rays of different colors are focused on different planes, causing colored halos around objects in the image.

chrominance
Hue and saturation information.

chrominance noise
A form of artifact that appears as a random scattering of densely packed colored grain. *See also, luminance and noise.*

close-up
A general term used to describe an image created by closely focusing on a subject. Often involves the use of special lenses or extension tubes. Also, an automated exposure setting that automatically selects appropriate settings for close-up photography.

CMYK
Cyan, magenta, yellow, and black. This mode is typically used in image-editing applications when preparing an image for printing.

color balance
The average overall color in a reproduced image. How a digital camera interprets the color of light in a scene so that white or neutral gray appear neutral.

color cast
A colored hue over the image often caused by improper lighting or incorrect white balance settings. Can be produced intentionally for creative effect.

color space
A mapped relationship between colors and computer data about the colors.

CompactFlash (CF) card
One of the types of removable memory cards.

complementary colors
In theory: any two colors of light that, when combined, emit all known light wavelengths, resulting in white

light. Also, it can be any pair of dye colors that absorb all known light wavelengths, resulting in black.

compression
Method of reducing file size through removal of redundant data, as with the JPEG file format.

contrast
The difference between two or more tones in terms of luminance, density, or darkness.

contrast filter
A colored filter that lightens or darkens the monotone representation of a colored area or object in a black-and-white photograph.

CPU
Central Processing Unit. This is the brains of a computer or a lens that performs principle computational functions.

cropping
The process of extracting a portion of the image area. If this portion of the image is enlarged, resolution is subsequently lowered.

dedicated flash
An electronic flash unit that talks with the camera, communicating things such as flash illumination, lens focal length, subject distance, and sometimes flash status.

default
Refers to various factory-set attributes or features, in the case of a camera, that can be changed by the user but can, as desired, be reset to the original factory settings.

depth of field
The image space in front of and behind the plane of focus that appears acceptably sharp in the photograph.

diaphragm
A mechanism that determines the size of the lens opening that allows light to pass into the camera.

digital zoom
The cropping of the image at the sensor to create the effect of a telephoto zoom lens. The camera interpolates the image to the original resolution. However, the result is not as sharp as an image created with an optical zoom lens.

diopter
A measurement of the refractive power of a lens. Also, it may be a supplementary lens that is defined by its focal length and power of magnification.

download
The transfer of data from one device to another, such as from camera to computer or computer to printer.

dpi
Dots per inch. Used to define the resolution of a printer, this term refers to the number of dots of ink that a printer can lay down in an inch.

DPOF
Digital Print Order Format. A feature that enables the camera to supply data about the printing order of image files and the supplementary data contained within them. This feature can only be used in conjunction with a DPOF compatible printer.

D-TTL
A flash control system that relies on a series of preflashes to determine the output required from a flash unit. The system does not monitor the flash output during actual exposure.

dye sublimation printer
Creates color on the printed page by vaporizing inks that then solidify on the page.

electronic flash
A device with a glass or plastic tube filled with gas that, when electrified, creates an intense flash of light. Also called a strobe. Unlike a flash bulb, it is reusable.

EV
Exposure Value. A number that quantifies the amount of light within an scene, allowing you to determine the relative combinations of aperture and shutter speed to accurately reproduce the light levels of that exposure.

EXIF
Exchangeable Image File Format. This format is used for storing an image file's interchange information.

exposure
When light enters the camera and reacts with the sensitized medium. The term can also refer to the amount of light that strikes the light sensitive medium.

exposure meter
See light meter.

extension tube
A hollow metal ring that can be fitted between the camera and lens. It increases the distance between the optical center of the lens and the sensor and decreases the minimum focus distance of the lens.

file format
The form in which digital images are stored and recorded, e.g., JPEG, RAW, TIFF, etc.

filter
Usually a piece of plastic or glass used to control how certain wavelengths of light are recorded. A filter absorbs selected wavelengths, preventing them from reaching the light sensitive medium. Also, software available in image-processing computer programs can produce special filter effects.

FireWire
A high speed data transfer standard that allows outlying accessories to be plugged and unplugged from the computer while it is turned on. Some digital cameras and card readers use FireWire to connect to the computer. FireWire transfers data faster than USB. *See also, Mbps.*

firmware
Software that is permanently incorporated into a hardware chip. All computer-based equipment, including digital cameras, use firmware of some kind.

flare
Unwanted light streaks or rings that appear in the viewfinder, on the recorded image, or both. It is caused by extraneous light entering the camera during shooting. Diffuse flare is uniformly reflected light that can lower the contrast of the image. Zoom lenses are susceptible to flare because they are comprised of many elements. Filters can also increase flare. Use of a lens hood can often reduce this undesirable effect.

focal length
When the lens is focused on infinity, it is the distance from the optical center of the lens to the focal plane.

focal plane
The plane on which a lens forms a sharp image. Also, it may be the film plane or sensor plane.

focus
An optimum sharpness or image clarity that occurs when a lens creates a focused image by converging light rays to specific points at the focal plane. The word also refers to the act of adjusting the lens to achieve optimal image sharpness.

FP high-speed sync
Focal Plane high-speed sync. Some digital cameras emulate high shutter speeds by switching the camera sensor on and off rather than moving the shutter blades or curtains that cover it. This allows flash units to be synchronized at shutter speeds higher than the standard sync speed. In this flash mode, the level of flash output is reduced and, consequently, the shooting range is reduced.

f/stop
The size of the aperture or diaphragm opening of a lens, also referred to as f/number or stop. The term stands for the ratio of the focal length (f) of the lens to the width of its aperture. (f/1.4 = wide opening and f/22 = narrow opening.) Each stop up (lower f/number) doubles the amount of light reaching the sensitized medium. Each stop down (higher f/number) halves the amount of light reaching the sensitized medium.

full-sized sensor
A sensor in a digital camera that has the same dimensions as a 35mm film frame (24 x 36 mm). Also often called full frame.

gigabyte (GB)
Just over one billion bytes.

GN
See guide number.

gray card
A card used to take accurate exposure readings. It typically has a white side that reflects 90% of the light and a gray side that reflects 18%.

gray scale
A successive series of tones ranging between black and white, which have no color.

guide number (GN)
A number used to quantify the output of a flash unit. It is derived using this formula: GN = aperture x distance. Guide numbers are expressed for a given ISO in either feet or meters.

hard drive
A contained storage unit made up of magnetically sensitive disks.

histogram
A graphic representation of image tones.

hot shoe
An electronically connected flash mount on the camera body. It is used to fire the flash and facilitate communication between camera and flash.

icon
A symbol used to represent a file, function, or program.

image-processing program
Software that allows for image alteration and enhancement.

infinity
In photographic terms, the theoretical most distant point of focus.

interpolation
Process used to increase image resolution by creating new pixels based on existing pixels. The software intelligently looks at existing pixels and creates new pixels to fill the gaps and achieve a higher resolution.

IS
Image Stabilization. This is a technology that reduces camera shake and vibration.

ISO
Industry standards from the International Organization for Standardization. When an ISO number is applied to film, it indicates the relative light sensitivity of the recording medium. Digital sensors use film ISO equivalents, which are achieved by enhancing the data stream or boosting the signal.

JPEG
Joint Photographic Experts Group. This is a lossy compression file format that works with any computer and photo software. JPEG examines an image for redundant information and then removes it. The data is rebuilt when the file is reopened.

kilobyte (KB)
Just over one thousand bytes.

LCD
Liquid Crystal Display, which is a flat screen with two clear polarizing sheets on either side of a liquid crystal solution. When activated by an electric current, the LCD causes the crystals to either pass through or block light in order to create a colored image display.

LED
Light Emitting Diode.

lens
A piece of optical glass on the front of a camera that has been precisely calibrated to allow focus.

lens hood
Also called a lens shade. This is a short tube that can be attached to the front of a lens to reduce flare. It keeps undesirable light from reaching the front of the lens and also protects the front of the lens.

light meter
Also called an exposure meter, it is a device that measures light levels and calculates the correct aperture and shutter speed.

lithium-ion
A popular battery technology (sometimes abbreviated to Li-ion) that is not prone to the charge memory effects of nickel-cadmium (Ni-Cd) batteries, or the low temperature performance problems of alkaline batteries.

lossless
Image compression in which no data is lost.

lossy
Image compression in which data is lost and, thereby, image quality is lessened. This means that the greater the compression, the lower the image quality.

low-pass filter
A filter designed to remove elements of an image that correspond to high-frequency data, such as sharp edges and fine detail, to reduce the effect of moiré.

luminance
A term used to describe directional brightness. It can also be used as luminance noise, which is a form of noise that appears as a sprinkling of black grain. See also, brightness, chrominance, and noise.

Mac
Macintosh. This is the brand name for computers produced by Apple Computer, Inc.

macro lens
A lens designed to be at top sharpness over a flat field when focused at close distances and reproduction ratios up to 1:1.

main light
The primary or dominant light source. It influences texture, volume, and shadows.

Manual exposure mode (M)
A camera operating mode that requires the user to determine and set both the aperture and shutter speed.

megabit
One million bits of data. See also, bit.

megabyte (MB)
Just over one million bytes.

megapixel
A million pixels.

memory
The storage capacity of a hard drive or other recording media.

memory card
A solid state removable storage medium used in digital devices. It can store still images, moving images, or sound, as well as related file data. There are several different types, including CompactFlash, SmartMedia, and xD, or Sony's proprietary Memory Stick, to name a few.

menu
A listing of features, functions, or options displayed on a screen that can be selected and activated by the user.

middle gray
Halfway between black and white, it is an average gray tone with 18% reflectance. See also, gray card.

midtone
The tone that appears as medium brightness, or medium gray tone, in a photographic print.

mode
Specified operating conditions of the camera or software program.

moiré
Occurs when the subject has more detail than the resolution of the digital camera can capture. Moiré appears as a wavy pattern over the image.

noise
The digital equivalent of grain. It is often caused by a number of different factors, such as a high ISO setting, heat, sensor design, etc. Though usually undesirable, it may be added for creative effect using an image-processing program. See also, chrominance noise and luminance.

normal lens
See standard lens.

operating system (OS)
The system software that provides the environment within which all other software operates.

ORF
The Olympus proprietory RAW file format.

overexposed
When too much light is recorded with the image, causing the photo to be too light in tone.

pan
Moving the camera to follow a moving subject. When a slow shutter speed is used, this creates an image in which the subject appears sharp and the background is blurred.

PC
Personal Computer. Strictly speaking, a computer made by IBM Corporation. However, the term is commonly used to refer to any IBM compatible computer.

perspective
The effect of the distance between the camera and image elements upon the perceived size of objects in an image.

pincushion distortion
A flaw in a lens that causes straight lines to bend inward toward the middle of an image.

pixel
Derived from picture element. A pixel is the base component of a digital image. Every individual pixel can have a distinct color and tone.

plug-in
Third-party software created to augment an existing software program.

polarization
An effect achieved by using a polarizing filter. It minimizes reflections from nonmetallic surfaces like water and glass and saturates colors by removing glare. Polarization often makes skies appear bluer at 90 degrees to the sun.

pre-flashes
A series of short duration, low intensity flash pulses emitted by a flash unit immediately prior to the shutter opening. These flashes help the TTL light meter assess the reflectivity of the subject. *See also, TTL.*

Program mode (P)
In Program exposure mode, the camera selects a combination of shutter speed and aperture automatically.

RAM
Stands for Random Access Memory, which is a computer's memory capacity, directly accessible from the central processing unit.

RAW
An image file format that has little or no internal processing applied by the camera. It contains 12-bit color information, a wider range of data than 8-bit formats such as JPEG.

RAW+JPEG
An image file format that records two files per capture; one RAW file and one JPEG file.

rear-curtain sync
A feature that causes the flash unit to fire just prior to the shutter closing. It is used for realistic portrayal of ambient-light motion blurs in flash photography.

red-eye reduction
A feature that causes the flash to emit a brief pulse of light just before the main flash fires. This helps to reduce the effect of retinal reflection.

resolution
The amount of data available for an image as applied to image size. It is expressed in pixels or megapixels, or sometimes as lines per inch on a monitor or dots per inch on a printed image.

RGB mode
Red, Green, and Blue. This is the color model most commonly used to display color images on video systems, film recorders, and computer monitors. It displays all visible col-

ors as combinations of red, green, and blue. RGB mode is the most common color mode for viewing and working with digital files onscreen.

saturation
The intensity or richness of a hue or color.

sharp
A term used to describe the quality of an image as clear, crisp, and perfectly focused, as opposed to fuzzy, obscure, or unfocused.

short lens
A lens with a smaller focal length—a wide-angle lens. It produces a greater angle of view than you would see with your eyes.

shutter
The apparatus that controls the amount of time during which light is allowed to reach the sensitized medium.

Shutter-priority mode
An automatic exposure mode in which you manually select the shutter speed and the camera automatically selects the aperture.

slow sync
A flash mode in which a slow shutter speed is used with the flash in order to allow low-level ambient light to be recorded by the sensitized medium.

SLR
Single-lens reflex. A camera with a mirror that reflects the image entering the lens through a pentaprism or pentamirror onto the viewfinder screen.

small-format sensor
In a digital camera, a sensor that is physically smaller than a 35mm frame of film.

standard lens
Also known as a normal lens, it has a focal length that approximates the length of the diagonal of the image frame.

stop down
To reduce the size of the diaphragm opening by using a higher f/number.

stop up
To increase the size of the diaphragm opening by using a lower f/number.

synchronize
Causing a flash unit to fire simultaneously with the complete opening of the camera's shutter.

telephoto lens
A lens with a long focal length that enlarges the subject and produces a narrower angle of view than you would see with your eyes.

TIFF
Tagged Image File Format. This popular digital format uses lossless compression.

tripod
A three-legged stand that stabilizes the camera and eliminates camera shake caused by body movement or vibration. Tripods are usually adjustable for height and angle.

TTL
Through-the-Lens, i.e. TTL metering.

USB
Universal Serial Bus. This interface standard allows outlying accessories to be plugged and unplugged from the computer while it is turned on. USB 2.0 enables high-speed data transfer.

vignetting
A reduction in light at the edge of an image due to use of a filter or an inappropriate lens hood for the particular lens.

viewfinder screen
The ground glass surface on which you view your image.

wide-angle lens
A lens that produces a greater angle of view than you would see with your eyes. *See also, short lens.*

Wi-Fi
Wireless Fidelity, a technology that allows for wireless networking between one Wi-Fi compatible product and another.

xD card
A flash memory card that is much smaller and lighter than CF (CompactFlash) cards; xD cards have metal connector contacts, instead of pins-and-plugs, so they aren't as prone to damage during handling compared with CF cards.

zoom lens
A lens that can be adjusted to cover a wide range of focal lengths.

Index